ARTIFICIAL INTELLIGENCE AND COMPUTER GAMES

ARTIFICIAL INTELLIGENCE AND COMPUTER GAMES

Richard Bartle

CENTURY COMMUNICATIONS

Century Communications

London

First published in Great Britain in 1985
by Century Communications Ltd
a division of Century – Hutchinson Ltd
Portland House
12–13 Greek Street
London W1V 5LE

ISBN 0 7126 0661 0

Originated direct from the author's w-p disks by
NWL Editorial Services, Langport, Somerset.

Printed by Billings & Sons, Worcester.

ABOUT THE AUTHOR

Born in 1960 in East Yorkshire, Richard Bartle is a natural games player; he was editor of his own games magazine *Sauce of the Nile* at the age of 14.

After graduating in Computer Science from the University of Essex he embarked on a PhD project involving cross-planning in Artificial Intelligence. In 1984 he became Lecturer there in Computational Modelling of Knowledge Structures.

He is one of the authors of MUD, the multi-user adventure game, and is chiefly responsible for bringing this exciting development to the attention of the world at large.

ACKNOWLEDGEMENTS

I would like to give my thanks to Gail Martin, who, at short notice, managed to proof-read the 2-inch thick wadge of computer lineprinter paper which at the time represented this book. Thank you also to the several thousand people who have, over the years, ventured into the land of MUD and play-tested it through all its many and varied stages of evolution.

CONTENTS

PROLOGUE

```
ESSEX UNIVERSITY: Multi-User Dungeon

This Mud created: 5th August 1984 at
22:01:57
Welcome! By what name shall I call you?
* galahad
What's this persona's password?
*
Yes!
Your last game was today at 16:24:24.
Hello again, Galahad!

Narrow road between lands.
You are stood on a narrow road between
The Land and whence you came. To the
north and south are the small foothills
of a pair of majestic mountains, with a
large wall running round. To the west the
road continues, where in the distance you
can see a thatched cottage opposite an
```

ancient cemetery. The way out is to the east, where a shroud of mist covers the secret pass by which you entered The Land.

* who is playing?
Galahad is playing
Lurker the necromancer is playing
Ciricio is playing
Osbert the warrior is playing
Rosal the heroine is playing
Oakes is playing
Altara the enchantress is playing
Richard the arch-wizard is playing

* A playful rabbit snuffles round your feet.

* get it
Rabbit taken.

* s
Foothills.
These are some foothills to the tall mountains which tower above you to the east. Travel in that direction is impossible because of a tall stone wall, built by the locals when they learned of the creatures dwelling within The Land... To the north runs an east-west road, and to the west is forest. The hills rise slowly to the south. There is a small hole in the ground, about 5 inches across. It bends too sharply for you to see anything down it.

* drop the rabbit in the hole
Rabbit dropped.
The bunny happily disappears into the warren, and you get a warm feeling inside that you have done something really worthwhile.

* score
Score to date: 137
Level of experience: Novice
Strength: 82
Stamina: 47
Dexterity: 68
Sex: male

```
Maximum stamina: 47
Weight carried: 0g (max. weight: 82000g)
Objects carried: 0 (max. number: 8)
Games played to date: 8

* s
Cave.
This is a cave, wherein once dwelled a
hermit in times long passed. Above is a
huge mountain towering amongst the
clouds, and outside can be seen a
pasture, small cottage and a cemetery in
the distance. At the east end of the cave
is a small opening in the wall. Lurker
the necromancer is here, carrying sack
brand mirror wand. The sack contains
something

*
Lurker the necromancer says "Hi,
Galahad!"

* lurker: hello!

*
Lurker the necromancer says "I haven't
seen you around here before."

* lurker: I only started playing a couple
of days ago

*
Lurker the necromancer says "So that's
why you say the commands in full instead
of abbreviating."

* lurker: what?

*
Lurker the necromancer says "It's quicker
to say DR BUNNY I HOLE."

* lurker: how do you know I did that?!

*
Lurker the necromancer says "I have a
magic mirror, it lets me snoop on what
you're doing."

* lurker: charming!
```

*
Lurker the necromancer says "Wait until you have enough points, then you can use it too."

* lurker: I'm only a novice at the moment

*
Lurker the necromancer says "I know. If you want some points quickly, try the goblin lair."

* lurker: is it near here? I've not come across it yet

*
Lurker the necromancer says "It's behind a portcullis, I'll give you a hand opening it."

* lurker: how far is it?

*
Lurker the necromancer says "Not far, follow me."

* lurker: if it's underground, I've not got a light...

*
Lurker the necromancer says "I have a lit brand, I'll give it you when we get there."

* lurker: why would you do that for me?

*
Lurker the necromancer says "Because then you will be able to see."

* lurker: er, OK

* Follow lurker
You have started to follow Lurker the necromancer.

* Lurker the necromancer has just left.

You follow Lurker the necromancer...
Before Gate.

You are standing in front of a huge oaken gate, rotted through over the ages so passage is easy. To the north is a narrow ledge over a deep pit, and to the south a dark passage whence drifts the scent of animals. The scene is visible by light beyond a smallish hole in the west wall. You can travel through the gate, to the east. Lurker the necromancer is here, carrying sack brand mirror wand. The sack contains something

* Lurker the necromancer has just left.

You follow Lurker the necromancer...
Before idol.
You are stood in front of a huge idol of a cyclops, hewn into the rock face and towering above you. To the west is a large doorway but the door has long since rotted away. Stairs run up the side of the idol to an opening at the mouth, and beyond. To the north is a small opening. High up the idol, embedded in its forehead, is a dazzling ruby for an eye! It seems to have remained there fixed for several centuries. Lurker the necromancer is here, carrying sack brand mirror wand. The sack contains something

* Lurker the necromancer has just left.

You follow Lurker the necromancer...
Outside mouth of idol.
You are stood by the mouth of a large and ancient idol of a cyclops. To the west, lower down, can be seen a tall but rotted gate. Above are the nose and eye of the colossus. A portcullis prevents passage east-west between the mouth of the idol and the opening to the outside. Lurker the necromancer is here, carrying sack brand mirror wand. The sack contains something

*
Lurker the necromancer says "Here we are!"

```
* open the portcullis
It's too difficult for one person to
lift. You'll have to get someone to help
you, from the same side.

*
Lurker the necromancer says "Not yet,
I'll help you."

*
Lurker the necromancer has offered to
assist you.

* open the protcullis
I don't understand that.

* open the portcullis
With your combined strength, the
portcullis raises!

*
Lurker the necromancer has given you the
brand.

* lurker: thanks! What now?

*
Lurker the necromancer says "Just
explore. I'm going now - cheerio!"

* lurker: wait, why did you do that for
me?

*
Lurker the necromancer says "So you could
find the goblin lair and some treasure."

* lurker: what's your name?

*
Lurker the necromancer says "Lurker!"

* lurker: no, your real name

*
Lurker the necromancer says "I don't have
a real name - I'm machine-generated."

*
Lurker the necromancer says "Bye!"
```

* Lurker has just passed on.

There is a sack here. There is a looking glass here. On the back is written the following: "If you have sufficient magical power, you may WATCH people. Break the mirror to stop." There is an ebony staff here without a rusty star on the end.

* get it all
Wand taken. Mirror taken. Sack taken.

* look in the sack
The sack contains doubloons

* look around
Outside mouth of idol.
You are stood by the mouth of a large and ancient idol of a cyclops. To the west, lower down, can be seen a tall but rotted gate. Above are the nose and eye of the colossus. A raised portcullis is above an east-west link into the mouth of the idol.

* in
Inside mouth of idol.
You are stood in the opening at the mouth of the idol. The walls are blacked with the incense of ages passed. An opening to the east leads deeper into the rock, whereas the mouth of the idol is to the west. A raised portcullis is above an east-west link into the mouth of the idol.

* quit

Duration of game = 12 mins 29 secs.

1

INTRODUCTION

1.0 ABOUT THIS BOOK

Upon picking up this book and thumbing through it, I anticipate there are likely to be two main reactions, depending on whether you know about computer games or Artificial Intelligence. The first of these amounts to 'Hey, get a load of all those mathematical symbols! This Artificial Intelligence stuff looks *hard*!'. The second is more like 'Aw no, computer games! And I thought it was going to be *interesting*'.

The point of this book is to correct both of these misconceptions. Artificial Intelligence (AI) is not a difficult subject once you get into it. Computer games are not a boring subject unworthy of serious attention. There are some very powerful programming techniques in AI which games programmers would love to use, if only they knew about them. Computer games are a very good application for AI research anyway, because they have certain features which are ideal focusing points for bringing together AI ideas. At the moment there is a massive gulf in the expertise which is available to AI people, and the dribs and drabs which leak out for consumption by the rest of the world. A lot of what may appear at first glance to the ordinary computer literate person an almost impenetrable collection of meaningless symbols and strange jargon words, AI researchers will find ridiculously simple, absolute novice stuff. As easy as the computer games fan will find the sections in this book dedicated to adventure games, say.

Of course it's fair enough to say that things *look* tricky, but that doesn't mean they actually *are*. Some of the sections may seem heavy going, and if so they can probably be skipped on the first time of reading (for example, the bit about the Predicate Calculus may blitz the non-mathematically minded when they first meet it!). However, if you have a logic programming language available to you, such as PROLOG, the chances are you'll find it much easier than you expected.

If AI and computer games are so wide apart, why attempt to bring them together? Because the resultant symbiosis can be absolutely devastating! For example, a program of which I have had a lot of experience, MUD, brings together ideas from both camps in a singularly effective way. It is thoroughly addictive, immense fun, and can run rings round ordinary computer games. However, it only scratches the surface of what *could* be done if the right people (you!) became interested in this mixing of ideas.

So this book explores some of the ways by which computer games, especially adventures, can be dragged out of the technological dark ages and into the AI revolution of today. It also points the way for AI people who have developed some interesting theories, and are looking for a sound, practical domain in which to try out their ideas.

Although I deliberately steer clear of references to either programming languages or specific computers, the details which are given in this book should be sufficient for anyone with enough time and programming expertise to go off and write their own adventure game program using AI techniques. Because of this original approach, it is easier to transport the program from machine to machine, to modify the program or write new games, and to write the game from scratch anyway!

Even if you don't want to write your own adventure, after reading this book you'll certainly have picked up a good background knowledge of both AI and computer games. Who knows, maybe you'll find yet another useful application for one or both of the subjects!

1.1 SPECIFICATION AND IMPLEMENTATION

When you're programming, you usually have at least a vague idea of what it is you want to end up with. This goal is normally called a *specification*. The process of writing a program to satisfy a specification is *implementation*. Sometimes you could have a fairly detailed specification of what is required of your program, perhaps even written in one of the semi-formal specification languages which are used in industry. If you've been given a list of things which the program must be able to do, say for example you were writing something to control robots assembling car bodies, then it's likely that your specification would be of this 'strict' kind.

Other times, though, you might have only an inkling of what it is you want to do, and set about trying to do it unconstrained except by your ability to overcome problems as they appear. If someone shouted across the room, 'Hey, you, write me something to play poker' then you'd only have a general idea of what's required, and your first attempts at a program could easily end in failure. More often than not, though, you'll be on a line somewhere in between these two extremes, where you have a pretty good notion of what it is you want to end up with and how to go about programming it, but you might not have looked into all the details fully yet. You may, for example, be programming some sort of financial package to sell to small businesses, and keep having to add in extra bits to keep up with your competitors. These extra bits may be tightly or loosely specified, and although the person who wants the program may have strong opinions with respect to the implementation of some of the things in your system, others may be content to leave it up to you.

Now although at the tightly-specified end much of the problem-solving part may have been done for you by whoever gave you the specification, there are plenty of implementational problems which can keep up your interest. As any hacker will tell you, it's a tremendous challenge to make your programs as efficient as possible (even if it takes you longer to figure it out than the total accumulated run-time you'd save by not bothering!). Rarely, however, will the task you've been given turn out to be impossible, forcing you to get the specification changed.

This can happen quite often at the looser extremity of the line, though. Here, progress is achieved by deciding what the problems are, and trying to figure them out. These 'problems' can be looked on as sub-specifications, if you like, and since you think them up for yourself it's OK for you to change them if you can't solve them. In your program to play poker, for example, you might decide to split the problem up into modules which deal out the cards, which assess the hand, and which bet. If it turned out that you then couldn't integrate these together, you might instead decide to split it into modules which deal out the cards, then assess the hand and bet simultaneously. Hence, although the problem may force you to write a 'hairy' solution, with lots of terrible ad-hoc components that make it just one big mess, you can simply adjust what is required so that obtaining the solution is made easier. You'll certainly have to do this if you learn that you were trying to program a solution to a problem which didn't actually *have* a solution!

This toing and froing between specification and implementation is what research is all about, and must be fun otherwise there'd be no-one willing to do it at universities! As your specifications become tighter, you move to the other end of the scale, and into implementational issues. These can still feed back to change what it is you wanted to do (you'd be in trouble if your perfect algorithm to predict the weather took a minimum of 25 hours to run), but it's less likely.

1.2 THE UNDERACHIEVER SYNDROME

It's easy, of course, to make mistakes in unconstrained, free programming. In particular, you can miss or overlook better (that is, more powerful or elegant) ways to do things, and end up with a program that's not as good as it might be because it goes about things the wrong way. I'll call this the 'underachiever syndrome', since the program could be improved if only it used its full potential. There are a couple of ways the underachiever syndrome can arise, namely finding a harder solution first and sticking with it, or not spotting a possibility which could relax some of the constraints you imposed on your solution earlier.

An example of the first way (often encountered in people who are starting to learn programming) is using a slow, needlessly inefficient linear sorting algorithm to get a list of numbers in order, simply because you hadn't heard about (or couldn't invent for yourself at the time) bubble sorts, quicksorts, shell sorts, or all the other sorts which knock the spots off a straight exchange sort. An example of the second way you can evolve a less powerful program, the case where the algorithm you're using is more general than you thought, is if you'd intended to write something which sorted integers but missed the fact that your solution could also sort strings; hence the end product isn't as good as it might be, through a missed opportunity.

This book is about two areas in computing where work is at the unconstrained end of the looseness spectrum. The first is Artificial

Intelligence, AI, a relatively new subject as far as university disciplines go, which involves lots of difficult, challenging, abstract research but with little in the way of practical results except for a myriad of programs which demonstrate how ideas are progressing, sort of tasters for bigger and better Things To Come. Impetus in the second area is very different from the laid back academic approach common in AI, since it is the highly lucrative computer games industry. Here, the best-selling games can net thousands for their authors. Not surprisingly, there is a lot of interest in this sort of activity, and many people are involved in it, although admittedly they're usually in close competition with one another.

Both these seemingly incongruous subfields of computing illustrate the underachiever syndrome. AI people have shunned any computer games except intellectually respectable ones (such as chess), treating them as merely toys, which are superficial, irrelevant, and not of interest. Meanwhile, they have toiled away on demonstrator projects to show their systems in action; these have no measure of cohesion between one another, nor any practical use. While governments pump millions of pounds, dollars and yen into AI research, hoping it will yield the fruits it promises to bear and become a useful tool for the industry of the future, the fact that it is needed by one of the fastest-growing industries of the present – computer games – has been missed. AI is of more general practical use than most people concerned with it realise. This is a real-life example of the second of the two ways in which the underachiever syndrome can happen; people are working in an area where they have certain ideas of what they want to produce, but don't figure on coming up with something else in the process. Their programs are better than they imagine!

With computer games software firms at each other's throats to produce the best products, commercial pressure to get things out fast is quite demanding. As most of the games written at present are by 'gifted youngsters' (although this is gradually changing), companies have tended to advertise for games, test play the hundreds sent in, and market some adaptation of the best. A few have formed teams of the more competent of these programmers, given them a set time to come up with a best-seller, and more often than not the programmers have obliged.

However, all work is done from first principles. The programmers do things in awkward, inefficient ways, or decide not to attempt something because they think it's either too hard, would take too long, or is just plain impossible. Their programs are suffering a loss of power due to these decisions, because it turns out that much of the work has been done already, and the techniques they require are well understood. Where they ought to look is in the AI literature. This is an example of the other way which leads to the underachiever syndrome, working something out yourself which isn't as good as something someone else has already made available.

Normally, in the software games industry, of course, people are very cagey about revealing how they go about things, so perhaps the people working there can be forgiven for making the assumption that everyone else is similarly paranoid. In fact, in AI there's a plethora of publications, with people falling over themselves to get their ideas into print! That's the whole point of research, so that industry can take up the better ideas and turn them into useful products, and the brightest academics can use this success (and the prospect of getting their names in lights!) to spur them on to further research.

1.3 BRIDGING THE KNOWLEDGE GAP

So it seems like all that games writers need to do is to read up the AI literature and they'll have at their fingertips a whole host of off the peg, ready-to-use ideas which they can plug straight into their games? Would that it were so! AI projects come as a series of incremental 'improvements', and there is a lot of background reading to be done in order to find out why the current favourite ways of doing things are effective. Also, to say that AI is a disorganised subject is rather an understatement: the naive reader, looking at the literature for the first time, is confronted with a mass of contradicting, detached and obscure ideas, and picking out the gems is nigh on impossible without having someone else tell you what they are. Anyone putting a sensible ordering on AI research topics could probably get a PhD for doing so . . . .

Also, although lots of AI is relevant to games people, a whole lot more isn't – rather like some electronics being relevant to computer people, but by no means all of it. There is an overlap of ideas, rather than the total subsumption of one set by the other. So how are those in the industry supposed to make use of AI when the AI workers don't recognise that they're there, and hence haven't organised themselves in a manner which enables easy access from the outside to cream off the best ideas?

One solution would be to awaken AI to the fact that there are a lot of people out there simply dying to apply AI methods to their programs, but who are finding it an impenetrable subject. The traditional way to do this is to offer researchers lots of money, but, since AI funding has been on the up-and-up anyway in recent years, that probably won't have as large an effect in the future as it would have done in the past. Besides, what is required is merely an explanation of existing techniques, not a whole set of newly-researched ones. For AI people to get hooked on research into 'popular' computer games there would have to be some additional reason for them to bother, something extra which would mean the subject was interesting in its own right. These people are in an almost unique position in the scientific academic world, in that they can pick and choose what to research with few financial constraints – their problems are primarily concerned with obtaining good people with whom to work. So some approach not based on money would be necessary to attract their attention. One such carrot which may tempt them into the games area is the mere fact that it's just tremendous *fun* writing this kind of program. Also, the ready-made application area means you can actually see your program *doing* something, and watch things happening as a result of its machinations. Of course, the AI bunch don't *know* this until someone tries it – and no-one will try it until they know it's worthwhile! Catch-22?

Well no, not quite. There are other ways to get AI expertise into the places where it's needed. First of all, you can hire individuals rather than try to sway the subject as a whole. This isn't as easy as it sounds, because researchers tend to be specialists in one particular aspect of AI, and may not know much about the various other mechanisms that AI has to offer but which lie outside their sphere. So you need to combine such people together in a team, under the direction of someone who has a sound knowledge of AI in general, and an appreciation of what it is you require for the end product. Only there aren't too many folk like that around at the moment – in fact the only way they can arise is if games is among their main interests, since otherwise they'd be researching studiously in whichever other areas they liked. The alternative is to be a games person and learn about the essentials of those aspects of AI which are relevant to you, but no more. The disadvantage here is that you need the same sort of person to instruct you as before, someone who can give you an idea of AI while understanding those areas in which you are interested, so as to cut away much of the deadwood. And such people are hard to find.

So the idea of this book is to build the bridge between these two fields, the theoretical (AI) and the practical (games). To the initiated AI researcher, it opens the door to an exciting new application domain which is *ideal* for integrating great chunks of the subject, and provides a solid platform for studying the interactions of the various sub-disciplines. It's terrific fun, too! To the reader who is *au fait* with computer games, especially adventure games, it reveals a treasure chest of new ideas in software technology, which should whet their appetite for whatever amazing systems they can expect to be experiencing in the future, as well as providing a fascinating insight into the fast-growing subject spearheading one of the last great challenges to human intellect – the mysteries of the intellect itself.

2
COMPUTER GAMES

2.0 THE HISTORY OF AI AND GAMES

To start with, then, I ought to describe the type of game for which I claim AI has so much to offer. I'll do this by way of a short history of the treatment of computer games, both in AI and in general.

Games have actually been part of the AI scene since its very beginnings. The general idea was that if you could get a computer to beat a human in a game of skill then the computer would have to have a bit of intelligence in order to do so. What better game with which to start than traditionally the most difficult of them all, chess? Initially, there were high hopes of coming up with a chess champion program pretty quickly, but it soon transpired that it was harder than it first looked. Still, perhaps that was even better, because in having to figure out how such a program was going to behave it would be necessary maybe to evolve techniques which could be useful in other applications, such as solving cryptoarithmetic problems, say.

Well that was in the 1950s, and things are still going on along those lines today. The trouble is that they're no longer of much relevance to AI in general, although they're very good for public relations reasons. Whoever first produced a program capable of beating the world chess champion would be onto a winner, and the interest it generated in AI would do the subject a lot of good. Well it turns out that there are programs around *now* which could probably do it. They'd probably need to take four thousand years between moves, but they'd manage it, eventually. You want a program to win in a shorter time? Well, just wait a few years until the hardware gets fast enough.

This 'if it beats a human it's intelligent' attitude is plainly wrong. Computers can do arithmetic millions of times faster than humans, but no-one thinks they're intelligent because of it. The fact that computers can win at chess if you put enough oomph into them should be enough to convince most people that even when a program does eventually beat the world chess champion it won't prove much about the superiority of machines over people. I'll talk about this later, however, since the problem is really at a deeper level than I'm making out.

Computers, or rather computer programs, already have beaten the best human players at backgammon and Othello (or, more properly, Reversi). Not surprisingly, a lot of the techniques to do this have been gleaned from the research into chess-playing programs. The reason for the success in these other two games and the failure so far with chess is because they are much simpler, there being generally less moves to choose between at any point in play. The oriental game go has also been studied in great detail, but as it can have more complex board patterns even than chess, human players win against go programs pretty easily. Like chess, the games Othello, backgammon and go were picked because of the respectability that they enjoy, since they are abstract in nature and are considered rather intellectual. There are notable programs which play other semi-respectable games, for example poker and bridge, but in general the big four have dominated this field (which is called *Game Theory*).

All the programs of this genre are fine at what they do, but they're highly specialised and have difficulty learning anything from how one particular game went in order to use the experience in the next one they play. There *are* programs which can do this kind of thing, however. One, called EURISKO, keeps winning the TRAVELLER tournament at the giant 'Origins' game convention in America – it's usually the only program to enter, all the other players being human. TRAVELLER is essentially a role-playing game, about which more later, but one aspect of it is that fleets of spaceships can be designed (within certain constraints), and then be pitted against one another. The Origins tournament organisers disclose to all competitors the amount of resources they will be allowed in the game to buy and set up their fleet. This is done some time before the convention, thus giving them a chance to work out their ideal set-ups. Then the resulting battlefleets fight it out in knockout fashion, starting each conflict from scratch.

Now EURISKO does this surprisingly well. It uses a set of *heuristics* (rules of thumb) to make observations about sets of rules, and generate new possible heuristics which might help it within those rules. So it might notice that small fast ships cost only slightly more than small slow ships, and decide it's a good thing to get the faster version of any small ships it wants. EURISKO does have other applications apart from games (something which none of the chess-type programs can claim to have), and hence is a program to watch out for in the future. Once the TRAVELLER rules for the Origins convention were announced, all the author, Doug Lenat, had to do was to program up some heuristics to capture them, and let the program rip. Every morning he would see how the program was doing, toss out all the junk heuristics which it hadn't disposed of itself, and let the machine run *all day*. No wonder it won, with that sort of computational power at its disposal!

Still, EURISKO really *is* a powerful program, and has produced lots of interesting results. It has also done some quite 'intelligent' things. For example at one point, having just generated a heap of heuristics that came to nothing, it formulated the generalisation *all heuristics I invent are useless, so get rid of them*. Since this was itself a heuristic, it promptly applied the rule to itself, and duly chucked itself away!

EURISKO is a development of an earlier program called AM, which tried to generate new mathematical concepts. It did manage some fairly powerful obscure ones, and came up with the odd well-known one from a surprisingly original angle. Most of its success was due to fluke, however, since the language in which it was written, LISP, had a lot of the features implicit in it anyway. What the designers decided were good lines of thought, being followed by the program on its own initiative, were actually nothing more than manifestations of what was inherent in LISP anyway.

There are many AI people who are very suspicious of AM and EURISKO, mainly because of the interaction with humans which is needed in order to make them a success. Translating EURISKO concepts into English is very difficult, and consequently the English paraphrasing of EURISKO's internal representations cannot be relied upon one hundred percent. It can't be denied, though, that the program is very good and useful, indeed it has already earned its keep by coming up with a new way to utilise silicon chip technology by using circuit components vertically as well as horizontally in their design. The version which did that was the same one which played TRAVELLER, but had a different set of heuristics fed in as its initial input. After working in electronics for some time, it had come up with new rules which were rather complex, and not of much use outside the silicon chip domain.

2.1 THE TURING TEST

EURISKO aside, however, few AI games programs have arisen which are not part of the 'Game Theory' line. There is another formulation in AI which also involves a game, but it has never been programmed yet. It was originally proposed in 1950 as an attempt to describe how to identify real Artificial Intelligence. These days, the name given to it is the *Turing Test*, after the British mathematician and father of AI, Alan Turing, who conceived it. Turing himself called it the *imitation game*, for reasons which will soon become apparent.

The scenario is that there's a man in one room and a woman in another, with you in a third. Communication is by typing notes on slips of paper and giving them to a messenger who delivers them. You don't know which room the man is in or which contains the woman, but you do know which room the messages you are sending and receiving concern. The goal of the man is to mislead you into thinking he's the woman, whereas the goal of the woman is to convince you that she's the real female. You keep on asking questions until you're prepared to guess who occupies each room.

So far this sounds just like some kind of Victorian parlour game, which is probably because it is one! Turing added a new wrinkle, as follows: instead of *man*, read *computer program*, and instead of *woman* read *human being*. The Turing Test is that if you're presented with a computer program masquerading as a human, and you can't tell by asking it questions and getting replies whether it really is a human being or not, then it passes the test and is 'intelligent'.

It's easy to arrange things so you can't tell the difference between human and machine in limited circumstances, for example you can restrict possible inputs by having only a small number of things which can be done. For example, you'd have difficulty telling whether it was a program that just drew a game of noughts and crosses with you or a person, simply because you can't really ask it (by way of making a move) anything which requires intelligence to answer. Suitable random-number generators could make the program play differently every time, and occasionally make a mistake. If you could ask the computer anything you liked rather than operating in a limited area such as noughts and crosses, then it would pass the Turing Test proper. So you could say things like, 'Who won the FA Cup in 1954?', 'What's the sine of 45 degrees?' and 'Tell me a good joke' one after the other, and hope to get plausible replies.

The Turing Test is rather an important notion in AI, and, as I hope to show later, in computer games. If you were playing a game with several other players at a distance (say over some network), then short of ringing them up and asking them you'd really have no guarantee that they *were* actually human beings! Not if the game could generate its own players, and these passed the Turing Test. As yet, however, no program *has* consistently passed the Turing Test, but there have been numerous fairly successful attempts in small, rather trivial application areas.

2.2 DOCTOR AND PATIENT

One such attempt which worked rather well was a program called ELIZA (after Eliza Dolittle, the waif who is taught how to talk proper in George Bernard Shaw's *Pygmalion*). This quite famous program pretended to be a doctor, specifically a psychiatrist, and utilised a particular psychological technique which is *non-directive*. In lay terms, this means that whatever you say to the analyst is said back to you rephrased as a statement or mild question.

Although ELIZA is old hat now as AI programs go, it's still quite impressive the first time you see it in action. The program seems to understand what you say to it, and gives a conversational response. Many people have been fooled into thinking there was a real person at the other end of the terminal, and yet others have treated the program as if it were a human even though they knew it wasn't. Legend has it that the secretary who actually typed in the program asked its author if he'd mind leaving the office when he walked in on her unexpectedly, as she was having a 'confidential' talk with ELIZA.

ELIZA, however, is easy enough to trip up. It works pretty mindlessly, looking for key words and paraphrasing around them. Although I don't intend to give a deep analysis of the program, an example might help. Suppose you said to it 'Bert is hungry'. It will match up in its collection of patterns and come across something like '?1 is ?2', where the '?' means it's a variable. Once it sticks the two together (a form of 'unification', which I discuss in some detail later for those who like to know such things) it comes out as '?1=Bert' and '?2=hungry'. It then selects the next response from the set list of responses which it associates with that particular pattern, and splurges it out. So if the next reply on its list is 'Perhaps ?1 really is ?2', it will change each occurrence of '?1' to 'Bert', of '?2' to 'hungry' and print out at the user 'Perhaps Bert really is hungry'. So far so good. The ?'s can mean more than one word, so 'Bert is very hungry' would get back 'Perhaps Bert really is very hungry'. Reasonable. If you give it something *really* challenging, however, it'll collapse. Upon being presented with:

That that is, is; that that is not, is not; that that is, is not that that is not.

the version of ELIZA which I have access to gave the remarkably obscure advice:

> Perhaps that that is is
> that that is not is not that that is is not
> that that is not
> really is is
> that that is not is not
> that that is is not that that is not.

Still, ELIZA does pretty well. It's quite fun if you indulge it with a modicum of 'role playing' on your behalf, for example talking as if you were John Wayne ('Gimme a shot of redeye, bartender'). ELIZA, however, doesn't itself ever take much of a lead in the conversation.

Another early AI program was one called PARRY, which this time took on the part of a paranoid patient itself, and you had to act as doctor. Here, things were slightly better because PARRY had good knowledge about a particular real-world subject, or *domain*, and could talk about it in detail using canned, yet human-like, phrases. The things it knew about were confined to horse racing and mobsters (which were 'out to get' the program, because it 'knew too much'). Because of this, the people playing with it were unable to ask it penetrating questions to catch it out, as in general it knew more about the subject than they did. If you tried to talk about anything else, it would come back to talking about 'the track', since, being paranoid, it was entitled to do this!

PARRY did meet ELIZA, of course, with quite an entertaining result. For my money, PARRY won the encounter, although there was some pretty meaningless conversation on both sides. For example, early on after being subjected to several of ELIZA's 'I am not sure I understand you fully' kind of response, where it couldn't match against any keywords so feigned ignorance, PARRY said, 'It's clear to me if not to you', to which ELIZA replied, 'Do you think it's likely that not to I?'. Hmm! At a later stage, it's PARRY that slips up with this exchange:

> *parry*: 'I don't understand your motives'
> *eliza*: 'Why don't you understand my motives?'
> *parry*: 'Shouldn't I be?'
> *eliza*: 'Why do you say that just now?'

Yes, that's what we'd *all* like to know!

The most entertaining part of the whole conversation comes near the end. PARRY has been consistently trying to make ELIZA talk about the races, gambling and so on, and has been admirably persistent. ELIZA has kept on asking the same questions again and again, though, which PARRY has noticed and become 'irritated' about, saying things like, 'You keep asking me about the same things, why not change the topic?'; 'I am getting tired of answering the same questions over and over'; and 'You harp on the same questions too much'. Finally, the following dialogue occurs:

> *parry*: 'In my opinion you have a one-track mind'
> *eliza*: 'What makes you think I have a one-track mind?'
> *parry*: 'I used to go to the track every week.'

Now that's what I *call* paranoia!

The reason PARRY is more effective is mainly due to ELIZA's endless pouring out of boring, similar, contentless sentences. Still, the idea of program playing against program, each thinking the other is a human being, is an attractive one, and one to which we shall doubtless return later on.

2.3 PARTITIONING AND INTEGRATING

There are other AI systems I could cite along the same lines, but they are all of the same low level of generality. No-one would seriously think that any of these programs was a human being for long if engaged in conversation with them, especially if the human was awakened to the possibility that there was a chance the other wasn't. Work in AI these days isn't so strongly directed towards a complete system which could pass the Turing Test, more to partial systems which have something to say about one particular aspect of intelligence or other. These partitions are areas of AI which have been identified by researchers as fields in which, to some extent, it's easier to achieve progress without interference from other elements of any unified model of intelligence than it is with these other ideas taken on board.

This is sensible enough, people don't make entire cars all by themselves in a factory, but the process is artificially partitioned off into sub-processes, and each of these use someone who's a specialist – expert in the skills required for that particular part of the overall effort. People who stamp out bodywork panels, for example, don't need to know anything about installing electrical systems, fixing on wheels, or constructing gearboxes. So it is with AI: it's hard enough working on one aspect of modelling intelligent behaviour, never mind all of them at once!

However, at some point you have to stick the sub-assemblies together and come up with your end-product. AI people have been reluctant to do this. The meanest of cynics might suggest that the reason is probably because if someone else got a close look at half of these AI systems the authors would be exposed as complete charlatans, but really it's probably because integration is too difficult. The problem of people writing programs which just don't match with other folks' programs due to their being written in incompatible languages is one obvious, but not insurmountable, obstacle. However, it's also pretty hard to come up with any suitable area of application where interests overlap, without going the whole hog and trying to design an automaton. The nearest thing people have so far devised to an integrated AI system is the 'automated office', and that's mainly because it's the sort of thing which impresses managers in industry, being just the kind of product they want, and hence helps to keep the money coming in!

The point is that if you want something to pass the Turing Test, you need to have an environment where humans and computers can 'exist' at the same time, and on an equal footing with one another. You need to be able to communicate in a fully-expressible manner acceptable to humans – ie. at least by typing in sentences, if not by speech. Lastly the program which is to pass the test must be required to do the same things as the humans are required to do, acting more in a sense 'with' them than 'for' them or 'against' them.

As you'll have surmised, the ideal area for this is computer games! But which sort? There are many kinds of game you can sit down and play (or stand up and play if you're in an arcade!); are they all of genuine use to AI? What about vice-versa? And does AI fit in with the trends of the future? It would be no use to the games world if it turned out that people preferred to play certain sorts of game which needed no 'intelligence' on the program's behalf whatsoever. It would be like, say, coming up with a great new fluid mechanics theory which revolutionised the construction of propellor-driven aeroplanes – pretty useless if they're soon all going to be jet-propelled!

2.4 THE COMPUTER GAMES PEOPLE PLAY

The sort of computer games which people buy for their own machines fall into three main classes. There are arcade-type games, adventure games, and the rest. 'The rest' mainly consists of computerised versions of normal, real-world games such as chess, hangman, Scrabble and the like. These traditional games were the first sorts written for computers, and some adaptation of them is to be found on most mainframe computers if you know where to look (which is usually in the same place as the lineprinter pictures of Snoopy, 1974 Dougal calendars, and half a dozen nudes!). Although dedicated chess programs still enjoy some success, in the main people don't bother with the others since the novelty wears off pretty quickly, and you can play the games they were developed from without using a computer just as easily!

Computers do, however, have certain features which can't be handled by pencil-and-paper or board-and-dice games, the most obvious of which are speed of processing and complexity of the 'board', ie. screen. These attributes are utilised to the full in the *arcade game* class, so called because most of them originated in amusement arcades. The first attempts were those crude, bat-and-ball tennis games, which can still be found in some of the more old-fashioned arcades along obscure seafronts, or in ancient pubs miles from civilisation. From these, there came a host of lookalikes – BREAKOUT, SQUASH, SOCCER et al. The whole scene really took off with SPACE INVADERS, where fast-moving actions and zippy graphics made the other games look so far behind it was almost like you felt they were clockwork and you ought to wind them up. SPACE INVADERS spawned its own clones – GALAXIAN, FIREBIRD, MISSILE COMMAND – and the 'set 'em up and shoot 'em down' sort of game was established.

Most games are now like this, albeit with different 'views' depending on which of the three dimensions has been faked (SPACE INVADERS, ASTEROIDS, RIP-OFF and the like are looking from the 'top'; DEFENDER, SCRAMBLE and co. are from the 'side'; STAR FIRE, BATTLE ZONE, STAR WARS, BUCK ROGERS and the rest are from the 'front' –

this is frequently given the misnomer '3-D'). The most sophisticated ones, for example ELITE (which is still an 'arcade game', although it's not to be found in any arcade), give you a choice of directions which you can scan. The only other major class of arcade game is the PAC-MAN series, whose 'walk the maze avoiding the meanies' strategy has proved a durable source of basic ideas for home micro games ranging from DONKEY KONG through HOVVER BOVVER to JET-SET WILLY. Flight and driving simulators make up the set of games of this kind.

The basic arrangement in all these arcade games is you have a screen with some entity on it which you're supposed to control. Whether this is a racing car, lawn mower, hunchback, First World War aeroplane, sheep, or something resembling a liquorice allsort, it doesn't matter. Normally there is a task set, which involves moving your entity from place A to place B, often with sub-tasks to perform en route, and usually with some malevolent obstacles to impede progress. Sometimes, all that has to be done is to eliminate the obstacles, whereupon you may get another 'wave' of them.

Although the screens in these games are usually quite complex, and there might be a good deal of thought required to play, the trouble with them is that when you look at what you're actually *doing* it's pretty trivial. It amounts to little more than hand-eye co-ordination, the sort of thing you get just as well by playing cricket or tennis, and when you really think about it it boils down to 'man versus random-number generator'. All that you have to do is to recognise some situation which the computer has thrown up at you, react to it within a certain time, and you're OK. The 'randomness' with which the computer decides when and what changes to make, for you to try and handle may be constrained by certain rules, but deep down what goes on is decided by a random-number generator. If it's not, perhaps that's even worse as it must then play the same game every time if you repeat your moves identically. The 'randomness' might be a genuine random (or pseudo-random) number generator, or could be keyed in to the clock so your moves 'determine' what happens next by its depending on the time at which they occur. It all amounts to the same thing though – the games are pretty mindless. If there were too much thought involved, they'd lose their fast-moving-action qualities, which make them so much fun to play!

Even though some of the above points may be disputed by certain arcade game die-hards, I think anyone would admit that the greatest failing of the games is that they slowly lose their magic as you become more and more experienced, until eventually your skill is only useful for impressing people who can't do it, in the same way as you might if you'd learned to juggle, say. At worst, the skills you spent so long mastering impress no-one, although this isn't going to be so likely in computer games as it could be in other pastimes (I was so proud when I first solved Rubik's cube!), since there are some people who find all arcade games absolutely impossible to play!

2.5 ADVENTURE IN ADVENTURES

The sort of game the 'serious' microcomputer owner buys is the *adventure*. The name comes from the original program of this type, where players explored 'Colossal Cave'; the program was called simply ADVENTURE (or rather ADVENT, since the machine upon which it took off, the DECsystem-10, only allowed six letter filenames!). This was the only adventure in existence for several years, until people who had played it finally wrote their own programs (ZORK and HAUNT, for example). It was still a good few years before adventures left the realm of mainframe computers and became playable on micros. Nowadays there are thousands of games of this sort around, and 'adventure' has become a generic term; if people wish to refer to the original game, they usually call it COLOSSAL CAVE. Most of these new adventures are absolutely hopeless, but the gems are quite excellent (THE HITCHHIKER'S GUIDE TO THE GALAXY, LORDS OF MIDNIGHT, VALHALLA and THE HOBBIT being generally regarded as market leaders at the time of writing, and with the micro versions of ZORK and COLOSSAL CAVE highly thought of, too).

So what is it that makes something an adventure game? Although there are a whole host of them around, their predominant characteristics are essentially pretty simple. The computer models a predefined world consisting of various locations all linked together. In these 'rooms' are certain 'objects', and the player takes on the role of one such object – normally some kind of swordsman or wizard, but occasionally other things, such as a tank or a fraggle. The player issues commands to the game in some restricted form of English, and these are acted upon in a predefined way. The commands do things to the objects, such as transfer their position from one place or object to another, or change a property (a *property* of an object being some fact about the object which is true). GET, DROP and GO are typical of the former type of command (GET and DROP move between the object the player is controlling and the room in which this object is located, GO moves the player's object to a different room); KILL is an example of the property-changing command, although to be excessively general you *could* regard the moving of objects as 'changing their position property', but I won't go into that sort of thing just yet. GET, DROP, GO and KILL comprise the basic core which is found in virtually every adventure game (along with a QUIT and/or SAVE so you can stop play without having to switch off the machine or get yourself killed by some obliging monster). Other pretty essential ones provide information, such as LOOK, INVENTORY and SCORE.

As a slight digression, I'll just mention that most players wouldn't actually consider what they do in the game as controlling an object by their commands. Those adventures which make explicit the fact by prompting with something along the lines of, 'What do you want me to do next?' rather than, 'What do you want to do next?' are generally regarded with disfavour. As far as the players are concerned, it's *them* out there in the world, not some puppet which is merely obeying their orders (although if the scenario is well set, by for example having more than one puppet, as in Infocom's SUSPENDED, this can be acceptable). The word 'player' can therefore be interpreted in two ways, one to mean the human being playing the game, and one to mean the object which is intended to represent that human being in the program. Which alternative is the one intended is usually pretty clear from the context. Most implementations don't actually treat player objects in the same way as they do other ones, and it's also usual to think of rooms as being something special rather than just a particular form of object, although I'll be going into detail about that kind of issue later. End of digression.

Although there are *some* random features in adventures, one of the salient characteristics of such games is that randomness does not play much of a part, being more for spice than a necessary and intrinsic essential of play. There are certainly few quick reactions required, although quick *thinking* might be. So although the cartoon-based arcade game DRAGON'S LAIR (which uses a laser disc for its excellent graphics) looks on the face of it an adventure game (you're moving this Dirk character around a classic, fantasy type of world), really it's not in the 'adventure' category at all. When you take away the frills, it's still with the rest of the 'push the button at the right moment' bunch. You might be obliged to do something at a certain time in a proper adventure, but normally you'll have a couple of seconds leeway either side of the ideal time in order to let you get your command in safely.

Adventure games are all about problem-solving. They normally involve having to move objects from one location to another to get 'points', until you get some maximum number whereupon you've finished. The alternative kind of objective frequently encountered is the 'quest', where instead of aiming solely to 'get all the points' you try to retrieve just one particular object – princess, stolen plans, artefact, or what have you – and bring it to a certain place.

Quest-based adventures are typically set in some detailed scenario to explain what it is you're supposed to be doing (this is called the 'plot'). There aren't usually any points in quests, you win all at once when you make it back with the holy grail or whatever. Plots in the 'get all the points' games can be less constrained, since no explanation of what you are doing is required except greed! Although the acquisition of points in these games is normally for moving 'treasure' objects to some predefined spot, you can often get them for reaching particularly difficult places, or for solving puzzles, too.

2.6 PROBLEMS, PROBLEMS . . .

Solving puzzles is what makes adventures fun. Stripped to the bare essentials, you can look on what you're doing like this: you're giving commands to an interpreter; these commands have certain preconditions – *boolean* functions (ie. they come up true or false) – all of which have to be satisfied before the command will work. These functions test the variables in the environment, namely where you are, what objects are present, and what properties these objects possess. As an example, say you want to move from one room to another. The body of this action is just to look at the room you're in and see which is the room in the direction you want to go, simply by examining the static (ie. permanent) information in the internal description of the current room, and retrieving the connection which you should follow. Your location pointer is then moved to the new room. You can't execute this body until you've satisfied the preconditions of the action, however. These might be that the door which links the rooms has to be in an 'open' state, and until it is you can't pass through it.

Hence it's clear that objects hold the key to the game, as they enable and disable the commands available to the player at any time. Only some of the most basic commands, like SCORE or INVENTORY, will have no preconditions. Even QUIT might not let you leave if you're involved in combat with something horrible.

As a more substantial example, it might be that you want to pick up a golden statuette but there is a troll guarding it. To kill the troll you need the sword, but that's in another room behind a locked door. Ah, but you have some keys! So you can unlock the door, pick up the sword, kill the troll and get the statuette.

This is a very general descriptive mechanism, and can be used to represent many concepts. The crucial thing is, however, that the world you are modelling must mimic real life quite closely. The player gets fun from finding novel but *plausible* uses for items. If you slip in a non-obvious 'magic' ability for some object or word, like maybe you can't open a door until you say 'I bid thee frong!' or an equally opaque phrase, then you'd better give a clue about it somewhere where the player can find it without having to know about *frong* in advance, otherwise it'll never be opened. The substantial example above loses all sense of meaning if the names of the objects are changed, even if the preconditions on actions which are enabled or disabled remain exactly the same. I'll show you:

'As a more substantial example, it might be that you want to pick up a balloon factory but there is a glass of water guarding it. To kill the glass of water you need the socket, but that's in another room behind a locked shirt. Ah, but you have some fruit! So you can unlock the shirt, pick up the socket, kill the glass of water and get the factory.'

See what I mean? The game functions in the same way, but is crazily unrealistic!

2.7 FULFILLING PLAYERS' EXPECTATIONS

The game in this form is unplayable. Unless there were sufficiently big hints around that the locals called all doors 'shirts', that a 'keywey fruit' grew on a bush in the Garden of Awful Puns, and the balloon factory was a child's toy one foot tall with a glass of water balanced so precariously atop it that you couldn't move from where you stood unless you recharged your atomiser gun at the nearest electrical point, then the whole thing would be ridiculously difficult. You need to cut down on the possible actions by using common sense and a bit of imagination. It's all too easy to ruin adventure games by making them too esoteric. If there are two hundred objects in the game and you need one of them in order to perform some task, then it's not going to be worth your while trying them all in turn, you need to find some *reason* why one object is more likely than the others.

The opposite approach can also spoil a game – making it so transparently easy or boringly mundane that it isn't any fun. 'Clive must reach the office by 9am. It's 8.30, and his bike has a puncture. Aha, here comes a taxi…'. It's not quite the same, is it? Even though that's the sort of problem people solve routinely all the time! Maybe that's what makes them want to play adventures? When you're solving tedious problems which are easy to recognise as tedious problems, all the challenge goes out of it. The skill in designing adventures is to make them so the player finds the game lifelike and exciting, although with an ever-present fear of the unknown. Certain relaxations on the real world may be necessary to add to the mystique of it all, such as magic perhaps, but these must be well understood by the players beforehand to exist. It's no use making people skip around in a world they know nearly everything about; they can do that in real life anyway!

2.8 THE MAKING OF A GOOD ADVENTURE

There are several things about adventures which can make or break them. Apart from the danger of the actions which one must perform in order to overcome an obstacle being too tenuously connected with the task to be considered 'fair', there are other features which Every Game Should Have but which, of course, few do! The lack of play-testing can ruin many an adventure, where actions which the player would have thought were perfectly reasonable are forgotten or ignored. If you tried something which you thought was quite nifty yet which came up with the 'I'm sorry, I don't understand that' kind of reply, then perhaps the fact that you'd come up with something that the person who designed the world didn't think of is consolation enough for its not working.

If, however, you tried something which you'd have thought was a pretty obvious thing to do and it gave with the same sort of canned response to tell you it wasn't in its prepared list of possible commands, you might be a bit miffed: 'Why *can't* I eat the biscuit?'; 'What's an axe *for* if you can't chop down trees with it?'; '*Surely* it will let me set fire to the paper?' If you get back a consistent reply which may or may not contain a clue ('You can't burn the paper, it's magic!') then you can feel happy, but if the program didn't even expect something like that to be typed, then you are justified in being discontented.

The outcome of making games work in this manner doesn't have to be *good*, of course, so long as it is 'fair'. If you're told a swamp is fuming and then walk straight into it while carrying a naked flame, you can hardly complain if the marsh gases ignite and blow you up, although you don't have to *like* the idea! So long as it was your own fault, you have to accept it, albeit somewhat grudgingly! If you did spot it could happen, and dropped your burning torch accordingly, and then later on it turned out that the adventure-designer had missed the possible explosion and you wouldn't get blown up anyway, you're likely to feel a certain sensation of disappointment at having wasted all that paranoia!

Adventure games can be made better in other ways, such as having fancy graphics. Some people (and I must confess that I am among them) prefer a text-only adventure to a pictorial game, in the same way that some people like to curl up with a good book rather than toddle off to the cinema. Often, graphics are just there as a gimmick, although others are genuine integral parts of the game, and contain clues which will have a bearing on what you do later on in the course of play. Aesthetic drawings can enhance a game, of course, like background music in films can help create an atmosphere, but the underlying adventure isn't really affected. There are those who might suggest it was a better game because of the pictures, but really it just amounts to window dressing. A chess-playing program doesn't play a better game of chess if you supply it with a little robot arm which can pick up the pieces and move them itself rather than telling you what move it wants you to do for it. It's a similar thing with adventures.

Whether graphics are a passing fad or not, I'm not sure. Certainly they will be superseded in the near future when laser discs allow proper, TV-quality images to be displayed instead of the rudimentary type of cartoons which dominate the market at present. However, there will be lots of graphics-based adventure games come out before then, because the long-experienced limitations in the amount of RAM available to programs are becoming less of a problem these days (a picture may be worth a thousand words, but that's almost 1K!).

2.9 ARTIFICIAL INTELLIGENCE AND COMPUTER GAMES

That completes my outline of computer games in general. So where does Artificial Intelligence come in to all this? Well, there are the 'Game Theory' sorts of games, but that subject has been just about flogged to death by AI people already, (which is a not-so-polite way of saying that it is 'well-understood'!). Arcade games don't really intersect with AI much at all, although some of the lower-level techniques might come in handy (for example efficient searching algorithms to make the aliens find out where you are in the maze more effectively than present methods facilitate). No, the real area where AI can be of terrific help to computer games is in adventures.

Adventure games and AI were made for each other. If it weren't for the stuffiness of the universities and the complacency of the games industry, this fact would have been recognised long ago! The signs were there for all to see, for example ZORK started off as a language understanding program at the MIT AI lab in America, and only developed into a game because its authors found that was just the kind of thing they required to provide a context for their program's vocabulary! Still, it's no use crying over spilt milk, what's needed now is some way for people to cross over the boundaries between the two subjects, and give us the games we deserve! Hopefully, that's where this book comes in!

So what will the symbiosis between the two produce? Will it be more of an adventure, like ZORK or THE HOBBIT, or more the Turing Test kind of game like ELIZA or PARRY? The answer is that it will be both! The basic format will remain that of an adventure game, but the AI influence will bring in a new element – people. The point is that if you want to make a program appear intelligent, then it must compete on the same basis as a human being in some domain. If you want it to pass the Turing Test, you have to allow more than one person in at once, so neither you nor the pseudo-people that the program has generated know at a glance whether they are communicating with a real-life person or something pretending to be one.

I hasten to point out that the Turing Test will like as not survive intact for several decades to come! The last thing I'm describing here is something which would be able to pass it convincingly, or to even approach that level of sophistication. The test is not designed solely to measure whether an entity is sentient or not, though; by studying the ways in which an attempt to pass it fails, AI people can gain a deeper understanding of the causes of the failure, and eventually a better insight into the nature of intelligence itself.

The reason I can predict with reasonable certainty what a coalition of AI theoretical skills and games industry practical experience will produce is because it has already happened! In only a couple of cases, admittedly, and both from the academic side of the equation so that the World In General hasn't yet been awakened to their existence to any great extent, but the evidence is still there. The two systems to which I refer are MUD and SMAUG. MUD predates SMAUG by about three years, but both systems were developed independently and both arrived at the same conclusion: if you want an adventure game that's out of this world, let more than one person play in it at once!

I shall be going into more detail about MUD shortly, using it as the basis for a generalised architecture of these advanced adventure games. Using this architecture, I shall then be in a position to demonstrate how AI tools and techniques can be used so you could, if you wanted to, set about writing a game yourself. The algorithms I shall describe will be high-level, which is to say that they're not the sort of thing you would find easy or efficient to do in an ordinary computer language such as BASIC or PASCAL. I will not be giving any space-consuming sections of code for you to stare at glassy-eyed and wonder what the hell is going on in them, but rather describe what happens in English and let you use whatever data structures and control organisation you feel appropriate for your implementation.

MUD, incidentally, stands for Multi-User Dungeon, and I shall be using the term generically to mean any of this new breed of adventure games. Hence MUD is a MUD and SMAUG is a MUD, but there aren't any other MUDS around for the moment that are well-known enough to be more than just rumours. The reasons I choose to do this are because MUD was the first of this kind of program (in the same way as ADVENTURE was the first adventure program), and because since 1980 I've been its maintainer and developer! The project was envisaged, and its core written, by Roy Trubshaw, from whom I inherited the program after about six months when he left University to make his fortune. MUD hails from the University of Essex, and SMAUG from Rutgers in the USA, but since the former is pretty difficult to access and the latter is as yet unfinished, you're unlikely to have played either. For this reason, I shall not be talking about the programs in great detail, but instead using the generalised MUD which I mentioned earlier as the basic structure to which I shall relate AI methodologies. Oh, in case you're interested, SMAUG apparently stands for 'Simultaneous Multiple AdventUre Game'!

2.10 BACK TO THE TURING TEST

To end this chapter, I'll return to the prologue with which this book started. This consists of a record, or *log file*, of a game of MUD played at Essex University, and everything in it is unchanged, ie. that's exactly how it happened (even down to the typing error!). Of course, it *is* carefully scripted, and I knew what I (as Galahad) was going to type before I started playing, but it does illustrate a point.

The Turing Test, as I explained at length earlier, is where if you can't tell whether something is a real human being or a machine acting like a real human being, then the result is a pass, otherwise a failure. Admittedly, MUD is a limited domain, and conversation is generally on game-related topics (so that you don't get asked things like 'What did you think of that Barry Manilow on the TV last night then?' – which is probably just as well!). However, it does provide a context where people are suspicious of everything, and where they might be on the lookout for computer-generated players.

Now a few years ago, people used to play MUD from the USA via the various networks and satellite links between Essex and America, before it became too expensive. One day, a couple of visitors came in to play, and one of them accidentally typed `log`, so his game was recorded for posterity (he thought you had to 'log in' to MUD). The two wandered around a bit, but kept being followed by a character called Niatram the Wizard (who was actually one of our computer operators who couldn't spell his name in reverse). After Niatram had killed them for no apparent reason a couple of times, the two became very nervous. 'Who's that Niatram who keeps following me around then killing me?' asked one, in panic. His more experienced colleague had obviously thought about this before, and replied, 'I'm not sure, I think he may be machine generated'! When Niatram next appeared, the two quit, to save him the bother of killing them. In multi-player adventures such as MUD, this confusion between people and program is actually quite common among novices. Niatram was, of course, perfectly human, or as near to human as computer operators can be.

So it is with 'Lurker' in the prologue. Lurker is me on another terminal, which may be pretty obvious but it still looks fairly authentic, all the same. That is not to say that it is impossible to write a program to behave like Lurker – quite the opposite in fact. It is one of the purposes of this book to give ideas as to how the construction of such a program may be approached. The design and control of these 'non-player characters' (as they are called in SMAUG, after DUNGEON AND DRAGONS; MUD calls them 'mobiles') is, in my opinion, one of the most exciting applications of AI ever to arise. After reading this book, I hope you'll think so, too!

If any of you really *did* think Lurker was a computer, incidentally, I guess that means I passed the Turing Test. Well, you couldn't tell the difference between a computer program and a real human being (and I *am* a real human being!). It's not only the case that computers can imitate humans!

3
KNOWLEDGE REPRESENTATION

3.0 WHAT KNOWLEDGE REPRESENTATION MEANS

Knowledge Representation is an AI term which, broadly speaking, means coming up with a coherent system for the structures which you use to keep all the information that your intelligent program needs. The storage medium your computer uses is pretty unimportant as far as knowledge representation (KR) itself goes, although the user would of course notice the difference between two systems with identical capabilities, but one of which used RAM and the other of which used cassette tape. This independence of KR techniques with respect to the machine upon which they are meant to be utilised isn't strictly the case, though; there are certain desirable KR architectures which might require specialised hardware, such as an associative (ie. content-addressable) store, and which would run so slowly on conventional machines that even if you *did* use tape instead of RAM, you probably wouldn't notice the difference. Incidentally, it looks like the human brain is just such a piece of specialised hardware.

The word 'knowledge' in AI usually carries connotations of *domain-dependence*. When something is domain-dependent, it means it only works in a limited area, either on a limited number of things or on only a small range of things. So a program which contains lots of heuristics on how to play chess is domain-dependent if the heuristics are pretty much useless for anything other than chess. 'Try to castle as early as possible' isn't the sort of advice you would give to someone who asked how to get from here to King's Cross Station. The rule is specialised to one particular application, and beyond that it is inappropriate. In its field, though, the knowledge is normally highly detailed.

It is possible, of course, to think of anything as domain-dependent if you look from a high enough point of view. 'Try to avoid horrible things happening to you' is the sort of rule you could say was domain-independent, it applies just as well to playing chess as to getting to King's Cross Station. There are some situations where the rule doesn't help, of course, for example if there were two horrible things about to happen to you, or if something horrible was about to happen to your mother. The more general you try to make the rule, the weaker it becomes. About the only advice which you can always give is 'do something, even if it's nothing', but then all human beings follow it automatically anyway, whether they like it or not!

So KR has to address the problem of being able to represent facts from widely differing sources. A good KR system should be able to cope with knowledge about swimming, cookery, British Steam Locomotives 1829–1853, Star Trek episodes, in fact just about anything. It should also be able to take the more general facts on board which could come up in several different places, such as 'The rule that if A implies B, and A is true, then B is true too'. Adding another piece of knowledge to the structure shouldn't greatly increase the time required to access any information; if, say, for every object you insert, you needed to make links to every other object in order to specify the relationships between the new object and all the rest, then your access times might grow exponentially with the number of objects added.

There are many, many representational schema which have been proposed in AI, but thankfully most of them are based on just a few classic notions, which express the guts of the idea. Everything else is just an enhancement, and is normally adapted to suit the particular needs of someone's system. So what are the KR requirements of a MUD? Before I can answer that, I have to provide the definition of a generalised adventure game, which will show the kinds of knowledge that can arise.

3.1 ARCHITECTURE OF AN ADVENTURE

I shall now describe what is known as a 'pseudo-machine' for an adventure. A pseudo-machine (or, equally likely, *virtual machine*) is an independent, hypothetical computer which can easily, albeit perhaps tediously, be implemented on whatever real-life computer you wish. That is, it is an outline of an imaginary, idealised computing engine which you could in theory build out of nuts and bolts and chips to run your adventure, but in practice you'd program up in whatever language you fancied and would instead run it on another machine which was already made of real hardware (ie. your micro, mainframe or whatever). You could look on the pseudo-machine as being defined by its interpreter, if you liked.

In order to explore the techniques afforded adventures by AI, a certain amount of time must of course be spent on discussing such games in general, outlining common features and illuminating certain concepts which are of particular relevance. Rather than go into details about any particular game, it's best to use the abstract model of a pseudo-machine to describe the 'ideal' basic architecture. This is because most of you will be unfamiliar with any individual game selected, and there are few commercial products, if any, which incorporate all the parts about which I wish to talk.

The architecture is described at a level above that of the implementation, since AI is itself a fairly abstract subject. Technical terms being introduced in the description are in italics, and are generally in common use (although some of the more specialised or obscure ones are gleaned from MUD).

To start with, then, assume the adventure is played by *users*. We'll allow more than one to exist in its *environment* at any particular time, hence it is *multi-user*. Users communicate with the *host* machine, running the *interpreter* program, over a network of some kind, or under timesharing, it doesn't really matter. The *database* is a program in some *definition language* which describes the environment, in terms of the *rooms* which make it up, and of their interconnections, and also what *actions* the user can perform, with the effects these actions have on the environment. Some of the *objects* in the environment are themselves capable of performing actions – these objects are *mobiles* (or *NPCs* – Non-Player Characters). The representations of the users in the environment are their *personas*. Some of the actions can have effects which don't occur until some time after the action is executed – such effects are handled by *demons*, which *fire* after a predefined amount of (real-) time has elapsed.

The database is *compiled*, from ordinary text into a form which the interpreter can understand, by a *loader*. This leaves a file containing the intermediate code – a *dump file* – which the interpreter can read in all at once at the beginning and then process. Because the interpreter doesn't know anything about the environment it will be simulating, it can't have anything *hardwired* in it which assumes the environment will contain certain things. However, many environments will share several aspects, and these are kept in a *library* of *get files*, which are modules that can be pulled in by different databases. Most of the *vocabulary* for adventures which have similar environments will be in such files.

The interpreter takes input typed by the user and produces textual output (possibly in addition to other things, such as graphics and sound). The input goes into a *buffer*, one for each user, which is *normalised* (by converting multiple spaces and tabs to single spaces, and putting everything into the same case), and then *tokenised* by looking the words up in a *lexicon* (or *dictionary*). This is then *parsed*, possibly using a hardwired *grammar*, in order to find out the meanings of words in that particular context. The result is matched with some representation in the vocabulary part of the database, and *executed*. This execution may be likened to a query request on a database management system – *DBMS*. Also required of the interpreter are mechanisms to activate and deactivate the demons (whether *global* to the game or *local* to a user or mobile). Numerous *front-end* processes are needed too, such as *accounting*, letting users *attach* to the game, handling *input* and *output* (I/O) for them and *quitting* them cleanly.

OK, lots of jargon words there! Don't worry. I'll tend to talk only about localised parts of the overall system at any one time, which means you only have to hold a few buzz words in your head at once. It's pretty evident what most of them mean anyway. So the basic control loop is that a user contacts the host computer where the game interpreter is sited, attaches to a persona and types in commands which are parsed into actions. This might in reality be done by the interpreter, or by a front-end program on a different machine, but it's not so important here how it's implemented. The actions which arise are executed, and changes are made to the environment as a result. Output is generated, and sent via the front-end to the user. More output, due to other users, the activities of mobiles, and demons (eg. it starts to rain) may appear while the user is assimilating/responding to the new information. The user only ever runs the interpreter, the loader and the database being out of bounds except to the people who design the games.

Several different games may exist. These are made up from different databases (except for some common *get* files) but are loaded by the same loader and interpreted by the same interpreter. This is a bit like the situation in conventional programming languages where you may have several wildly different PASCAL programs which have a shared set of *include* files, and which are compiled into some intermediate *p-code* by the compiler, and then interpreted by the interpreter.

3.2 SOME THOUGHTS ON THE ARCHITECTURE

Although this isn't strictly to do with knowledge representation, it is worth providing a few reasons for some of the decisions made with respect to the pseudo-machine which I have just described. Of course, although I've deliberately tried to steer clear of implementational issues, there is a strong dependency between specification and implementation, and some of the features described are as a result of vague assumptions about the implementation, which I'll now come clean and admit!

It is apparent from the preceding set of definitions that the architecture is just a skeleton, which needs to be fleshed out in any particular implementation. There are plenty of questions arising from it, however, some of which are implementational and others which are higher-level. The lower-level ones will not, in general, be addressed here, even though in practice they might be quite important. How are the players connected together? A network? A ring? Timesharing? On what sort of computer is the game resident? A mainframe? A mini? A collection of micros? Or some other arrangement, say a mini with another one as a front end? How do you do things like stop several people from updating the environment at once?

The questions likely to arise at the higher level are more interesting, particularly from the AI standpoint. How is the parsing done? How do you represent actions in the database? How do you represent the environment itself? How do you make the mobiles behave sensibly? What do you do if a command is ambiguous?

A few of the low-level decisions impinge on the rest of the architecture. The reason the normalisation isn't necessarily performed by the parser, for example, is so that you could maybe get the user's micro to do it for you if they were playing over some kind of network. Similarly, the higher-level decisions mean that some low-level solutions are suggested, in that maybe the multi-user aspect (put in to make Turing Testing easier) would perhaps interest someone owning a network, or cable TV set-up; this is because such systems are presently the only ones which promote interaction between users, and any software exploiting this could open up new markets. Front-end processing can be done by the host or a different machine, due to the modularity.

Commercially, such a system would be quite appealing. Users can have a choice of games to play, due to the possibility of having different databases. This is made easier if the database definition language is well-constructed, and modules may be shared between them via the get files. If a network approach is taken, the users don't get a chance to pirate the software because all they ever do is play the game. They have no access to the loader or the database definitions, and even if they did they would need a network of their own and possibly some quite hefty computers (depending on the size of the game) before they could do anything with it. They would not give away passwords to friends, because if they had been playing a while and their persona was quite powerful, the friend could easily get it killed by accident, and the user to whom it belonged would then have to start from scratch. Besides, there's a feeling of 'it's me out there!' which people are reluctant to give up when someone else taints their persona.

The reasons for having an interpreter, and not programming the game directly in some ordinary programming language, are portability and modularity. Modularity means you can take great chunks of one database and include them in another by using the get files, something which is less easy to do in normal languages because unless you have database independence, the various procedures get small hacks creeping in to cover special cases. Portability means that if you want the game to run on another computer, or maybe even a different configuration of machines of several types, the database need not be rewritten, only the interpreter. This means that as far as the person who designs the environment is concerned, the program is going to work the same no matter what system it runs on. That's the beauty of using a pseudo-machine.

So this rough discussion on the feasibility of the implementation of the architecture is about all I have to say of things at that level. From now on, the concern is only with the implementation-independent concepts, namely general mechanisms relating to such weighty concepts as understanding sentences, making the mobiles react to events, and the design and use of the definition language. All this would be useless, of course, if you couldn't keep the environment in a form amenable to the changes you wish the actions to make, yet powerful enough to express all the sorts of notions you'd typically want in adventures. That brings us back nicely to the subject of knowledge representation, and hopefully some real, live, raw AI!

3.3 WHAT ADVENTURE GAMES REQUIRE OF KR SYSTEMS

Knowledge representation depends to quite an extent on what the knowledge is that you wish to represent, which isn't altogether surprising. However, there are several simple yet powerful forms which are adaptable enough to cope with most, if not all, of the specific structures which are likely to crop up in any KR application. Mathematically they're equivalent, which is to say you can map representations in one system over into another one with mechanistic ease. Each KR technique has its own advantages and disadvantages depending on how you wish to use the knowledge, and how it's structured. So what do adventure games, and MUDs in particular, ask of a system?

Well first let's just consider the environment, the fantasy (or otherwise!) world which you create for people to wander around in. Obviously they're going to want a real-time response, so better make it fast-access. It must be easy to update, in the sense of changing the positions of items relative to each other, but whole-scale construction of new entities (rooms, players, objects etc) is not required except when the database loader first builds up the main structure. This is done 'off-line', so it can be relatively slow.

Should the whole system be homogenous? In other words, should all entities in the world model be represented by adaptations of the same structure, or should any individual specialities they exhibit be exploited, and their own, custom-built representations used? MUD, for example, used different and incompatible data structures for players, rooms and objects. This was as a result of an implementational constraint to save on space, but the partition exists in most adventure games, even ones with no memory problems. The reason, it would appear, is because that makes them easier to program. If you try to keep everything too general, it can get on top of you. Besides, why would you *want* a homogenous system? Players, objects and rooms are entirely different things! Aren't they?

As I pointed out earlier, there is a fair amount of resistance to considering players as the same kind of thing as 'objects', people like to think it's them in there, existing in a real, albeit strange, land. However, there is a great deal of similarity between the things which make up an environment. Ordinary objects don't look like players, but what about the mobiles? They wander around like players do, can perform quite sophisticated tasks, and even perhaps possess a rudimentary communicative ability. Anything players can do, in theory they can too. So the distinction blurs there. And what about rooms? Well rooms are just a generalisation of a particular kind of object, a ‘container’. An old sack can hold doubloons and pieces of eight, a room can hold the old sack, Fenwyn, and a dead rabbit.

Rooms are joined together in a network of nodes, which means the environment roughly approximates a ‘state-to-state diagram’. This is a mathematical tool for describing computations and algorithms: it amounts to saying that you can describe any ‘computable’ function on a state-to-state diagram, which is a network of nodes (states) with arcs going off to other nodes. Each arc is labelled, so if you were at state **A** in Figure 3.1, say, which links to states **B**, **C** and **D** with arcs labelled **a1**, **a2** and **a3**, then when you look at the next input you compare it with the arcs and if it was **a1** you go to state **B**, **a2** to **C** and **a3** to **D**. Your final destination is a function of where you started and what you said. The similarity with the ‘travel table’ in an adventure should now be obvious: the states are ‘rooms’, and the arcs are labelled with directions. The reason I'm mentioning this in such detail is because state-to-state diagrams come up later on in the book under several different names, and I wanted to make use of a handy metaphor so you'd understand them better when it happened!

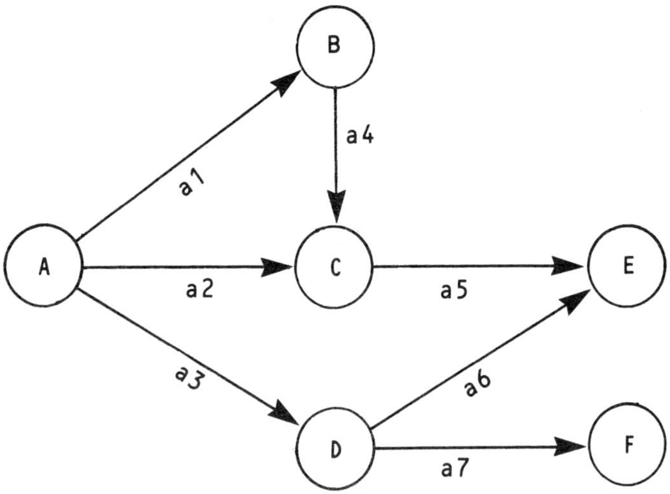

Figure 3.1 State-to-state diagram

This network is a relationship between entities, all the same. It is not, however, affected by other states of affairs. It's quite sensible to have all the rooms in the environment 'contained by' some other room, say one called 'universe'. Some small sections might be 'inside' more ordinary objects, so you could have a magic bottle which you carried around and which contained thirty rooms that you could enter if you shrank yourself to half an inch in height and jumped in the bottle. You could in theory do whatever you liked to these rooms, they're just like objects – and hence the blurred distinction comes in again. There should be no practical reason why you couldn't remove rooms, and maybe drop them elsewhere, perhaps inside other objects or rooms, or do any other things like that. It's reminiscent of the nested directories in a structured file-store actually being files themselves. However, one relationship between the rooms which you cannot readily change using the normal get, drop, insert, remove type of action is the state-to-state link. No matter where the East Pasture is placed in the database – inside 'universe' or inside a tin of soup – going west from it should always take you to the same place, the West Pasture, say. The reason is that what you carry is a list, a flat structure, and adding a new element to it just sticks it at the front or the back. There's no sense of the new element being 'west from' any of the other elements in the list.

For this reason, I'm prepared to accept that for the travel table it's pretty safe to use a different data structure, unless you actually want to be able to change the position of rooms with respect to one another, of course, by earthquakes or something. However, the rest of the system should use a homogenous representation, ie. there is no distinction between an object and a player, except that they might have different properties in some respects (players will all be 'containers' but not all objects will be; some objects might be radioactive, but no players will be).

It'll turn out, as we shall see, that the mechanisms I am about to describe are sufficiently general to be able to incorporate the travel table anyway. Indeed, they should be able to cope with the vocabulary, too, so that the same representation can be used for the environment and for the changes which have to be made to it as a result of typing DROP VASE or whatever. So there's no translation problem, the vocabulary's representation of what it means to be a vase is the same as the database's.

Generalisation like this has a bad name in AI, too many systems have been built which claimed to be the universal panacea but which were unable to live up to their promises. This is because there are domain-specific problems in most applications which require them to be used in a clumsy or unnatural fashion. Anything involving continuous quantities, such as time or space or light, is a big headache. In adventures, though, these are all quantised. No-one objects to having 'rooms' rather than a pair of co-ordinates to describe their current position, although co-ordinates may be useful to work out what was affected by an explosion, say. It would be tedious to be told that you were walking down a passageway and were 15 yards from one end and 8 from the other. You want to be able to regard the passage as a whole entity, and if it has interesting sub-parts well they ought to be rooms in their own right instead of merely being a set of co-ordinates. Similarly, time in adventures, especially multi-player ones, works by clock ticks. Things can never happen truly simultaneously if they're run on one computer or they wish to access the same memory (implementational issues making their mark again) so time is 'discrete' rather than continuous. Hence, many of the domain-specific problems which are the bane of programs purporting to be 'general' simply don't arise in MUDS.

3.4 THE FRAME PROBLEM

I'll start the discussion of real AI KR, by explaining the biggest difficulty facing anyone who wishes to model some environment on a computer: the so-called *Frame Problem*. The word *frame* has two meanings in AI. We'll be coming across one meaning presently. The meaning here, though, comes from a metaphor which compares the program or simulation to a cartoon animation film at the cinema: when the film is rolling, the action looks continuous to the viewer, although it actually consists of a number of 'frames', each one almost identical to the previous one, but with a few tiny changes. If there are not many frames to the second, some of the quicker actions carried out by the cartoon characters will look a little jumpy. Where there are more frames per second it'll look better, but there will still be some things happening in between frames which the viewer will miss. The more detail you want to take into account, the more expensive it becomes, and the faster the machinery you need. Of course, beyond a certain speed no-one is going to notice anything anyway, and that's where the analogy ends. However, you can hopefully see what would happen: the more detail you go into, the more things you can see, but you can never get *all* the details because frames are discrete and time isn't (well, we think it isn't!). Anyway, that's the cinema model, with what does it correspond in the programming world?

Translated directly into our terms, the problem is, on the face of it, how much detail you go into when you try to represent actions. Actions can be thought of as follows: they take a description of the world (a snapshot, or 'still', if you like), and from it produce a new description, or perhaps a sequence of new descriptions which describe the world through various stages of the action's execution. So `leave room` as an action might have an initial state of the world where you're in the middle of the room, then a second state which has you by a closed door, then a third where you're by an open door, and finally a fourth in which you're outside the room (and an open door). Each of these phases is a bit like a frame in a movie, and one phase is just like the previous one except for a few little changes.

The problem which now faces the person trying to describe the actions, who is known as the *knowledge engineer*, is to decide what these changes ought to be. How fine-grained should an action be in a MUD? If I were to `open door with keys` then is that a two-phase process, where first the door is unlocked (but still closed), then secondly it's opened wide? Or is it a one-stage process that has it happening all at once? It might be significant: if the door was jammed or held shut, then in the first implementation it would end up shut and unlocked, in the second it would be shut and locked. It sounds, then, that more detail is what you want and you might as well put it in to make your program more realistic. That's not actually the case, however.

To extend the cinematic analogy, with a really expensive camera, lots of professional animators, and even more frames per second of film, then the changes between them would be even smaller, but that of course means that tinier details come to light. We could make the door-opening action have three steps: hold the key in your hand, turn it in the lock, push the door open. Then if the door didn't have a keyhole you'd end up with the key still in your hand. In the other cases, this 'hand' isn't even mentioned. Good idea then? Well no, because it's *you* who has to program this system, and these tiny details interact with each other no end. Now we have the concept of a hand and there are loads of other things you can do with hands apart from open doors with them. So now you have to put all of those in, too. And why stop at hands? What about fingers? Muscles? It goes on far deeper. So the finer the detail you take, the greater the number of effects which come up as a result of your actions. This is the crux of the Frame Problem.

You can never really work out the full consequences of what you do, of course, you just hope that they peter out after a bit and are mainly local. When I breathe, for example, air currents are set up. Occasionally, these currents may cause something to happen which somebody else might notice, as they would if I directed breath at a nearby candle and it went out, but more often than not they won't be *aware* of any change. However, their environment is subtly changing as a result of my breathing – who is to say *what* minute influences it has on other things? A piece of dust disturbed by my breath could work its way into someone's nostrils and make them sneeze. Pollen in the air could then be carried onto a flower in my vicinity and fertilise it. There will be a slight temperature increase which *could* be just that fraction of a degree extra required to set off a fire alarm. Normally of course you don't bother even to think about the consequences of your breathing – more the consequences of your *not* breathing! You *can* think in more detail if you like, which is the equivalent of taking more Frames, but then you get more consequences following up. What is the effect of the blink of my eye on the price of tea in China? There *must* be *some*, surely?

In programming terms, then, the problem facing the environment designer is how deep to go. If you go too deep descriptively, the program forever spends its time doing 'domino effect' actions, where each little thing has a consequence which causes something else which causes something else and so on. If you don't go deep enough, the whole point of the exercise vanishes – you might as well have one action, `win`, which does everything for you. The Frame Problem is the single biggest difficulty facing the knowledge engineer. The lack of detail carries the danger of trivialising the task, but an excess just makes things tedious.

What would be nice, naturally, would be to have a system which can select the grade of film required as dictated by the circumstances. So fast-moving action gets lots of Frames, slow stuff gets the bare minimum before you can see the gaps. Hence a program which could determine that something is difficult for one person and give them all the details, whereas for another player who is differently skilled only produce the important stuff and forget the rest, would be quite a boon. This sort of program does exist, in a sense, in the part of AI called planning, where such 'levels of abstraction' are used quite often, for example to describe a task for the user to do, and if they don't understand it (or botch it up), then go to the next level of detail to explain it all. Even this method doesn't get round the Frame Problem, though, because you still have to design the world model so that it handles the deepest level of abstraction all the time. Although the player can use higher-level commands, you still have to follow up all the details. So whether you are told `open door with keys` or `get keys`, `unlock door with keys`, `open door`, you still have to do the same primitive actions.

So why wouldn't you want to do that? A little detail never hurt anyone did it? Well you wouldn't want to because you can keep on splitting, taking finer and finer Frames, down to the atomic level and beyond if you like! You'll still not get it exactly right. The trouble is, the *real* universe manages to do it all automatically, without 'thinking' of the cause and effects of actions, they just happen simultaneously and it gets on with it; you the programmer have to work out all the effects of the actions, and how they change the environment and possibly spark off new effects. That's when you think about hiring a physicist to help!

4
FORMAL LOGICS FOR KNOWLEDGE REPRESENTATION

4.0 THE PROPOSITIONAL CALCULUS

Let's take a look now at some classic types of KR techniques upon which most of the others are based, and see whether they're any good for MUDS or not (and, of course, say why). The main one which I intend to describe is called the *Predicate Calculus*. Hmm, sounds quite technical doesn't it? It's based on the *Propositional Calculus*, which, although it sounds even more pompous, is actually quite simple. So simple, in fact, that most people know it already (although they don't necessarily *know* they know!). The Propositional Calculus isn't too much to do with KR, but I'll detail it here because then you'll have no excuse for not understanding the basics of the Predicate Calculus, when it is discussed shortly!

In the Propositional Calculus, as with any other logic, the most important idea is that of truth (ie. true or false). You make a list of statements in the calculus, all of which have a value of true or false. Normally, things you state are taken to be true. So you might be able to say 'the bag contains the herb' or 'Bert is carrying the horse' or 'seven people weigh 600kg'. These are called *propositions*, and are complete entities in their own right (ie. they mustn't be broken down into pieces). Each one of them is a proposition, and is 'atomic'. Whether a proposition is true or not depends on nothing except whether you've *said* it's true or not. Since it has no formal relationship with English, the English meaning doesn't have to be sensible, so 'seven people weigh 1kg' is just as good a proposition, but it happens to be false if you interpret it in English.

Usually, though, to make them easier to understand, propositions are worded so that they coincide with their English meaning, which is to say that you needn't worry *too* much about it! However, you can't make deductions from the English meaning of a proposition either: 'Alice can touch the ox' tells you *nothing* about how close Alice is to the ox; 'Desmond and Ursula are siblings' is just a proposition, you can't infer from it that they have the same parent. So propositions are all those things we can say are true or false, and things like 'Cecil's height' and 'the speed the seagull flies at' are not propositions because they can't have a truth value associated with them (ie. these, and things like 'the tile on the roof' don't have a value of either true or false).

Individual propositions like this are pretty boring, they get better and more meaningful when you join them together. There are several ways to do this, using what are called, 'sentential connectives' in the language of the logician. The ones with which you'll be most familiar, and their usual symbols, are '`and`' ('∧' or '`&`'), '`or`' ('∨' or '`|`'), '`not`' ('~'), '`implies`' ('`=>`') and '`is equivalent to`' ('≡'). Using these sentential connectives with propositions gives us the Propositional Calculus.

So examples of use might be 'the sword is in the bag `or` it is in the sack' (which uses '`or`'), 'the meat is on the table `and` the table is on the floor' (which uses '`and`') and 'if the poker is in the flame, then it is hot' (which uses '`implies`'). The meaning of each of these connectives is supposed to be the same as in English, but to make things clearer (especially for '`implies`') I'll list them out here.

P∧Q
If both of propositions P and Q are true, then P∧Q is also true. Otherwise one or both are false, and P∧Q is false.

P∨Q
If either proposition P is true or proposition Q is true or they are both true then P∨Q is true, otherwise they're both false, and P∨Q is false. This is sometimes called *inclusive or*, as opposed to the *exclusive or* which means P is true or Q is true but not both.

~P
If proposition P is true then ~P is false, and if proposition P is false then ~P is true.

P=>Q
Well, this one *isn't* so simple! It's supposed to mean 'if P is true, then Q is true', and is the sort of thing people use all the time ('if you kick me on the shin, then I will pull your arm off'). So what's the truth value of the connective P=>Q itself? It's defined to be true if Q is true or P is false, or if you prefer it said the other way, false only if P is true and Q is false. Don't worry for the moment if you find that odd, '=>' is indeed a strange animal.

P≡Q
If P has the same truth value as Q then P≡Q is true. If they are both different, it's false.

To illustrate these with examples, I'll lapse into English for a while. Let's have four propositions which we'll use, 'Bimbo is a dog', 'Bimbo is not a dog', 'Bimbo has a tail' and 'Bimbo hasn't a tail'. The first and third we'll say are true, and the other two are false. So to make them formal propositions in the Propositional Calculus, we'd say:

Bimbo is a dog
Bimbo has a tail

~Bimbo is not a dog
~Bimbo hasn't a tail

OK, let's show '∧' in action:

Bimbo is a dog ∧ Bimbo has a tail is ***true***
Bimbo is a dog ∧ Bimbo hasn't a tail is ***false***
Bimbo hasn't a tail ∧ Bimbo has a tail is ***false***
Bimbo is not a dog ∧ Bimbo hasn't a tail is ***false***

That was pretty obvious, now for '∨':

Bimbo has a tail ∨ Bimbo is a dog is ***true***
Bimbo is a dog ∨ Bimbo hasn't a tail is ***true***
Bimbo is not a dog ∨ Bimbo is a dog is ***true***
Bimbo hasn't a tail ∨ Bimbo is not a dog is ***false***

And now for '~':

~Bimbo is a dog is ***false***
~Bimbo hasn't a tail is ***true***

The funny one – '=>':

Bimbo is a dog => Bimbo has a tail is ***true***
Bimbo is a dog => Bimbo hasn't a tail is ***false***
Bimbo is not a dog => Bimbo has a tail is ***true***. It might as well be since our propositions say that 'Bimbo is not a dog' is false anyway. The implication is essentially irrelevant, since it never 'applies'!

Bimbo is not a dog => Bimbo hasn't a tail is ***true***. We know that 'Bimbo is not a dog' is false, so whether the fact that 'Bimbo hasn't a tail' follows from that or not isn't of much importance really (even if Bimbo indeed has a tail, but is a peacock rather than a dog). Many people find this 'counter-intuitive' (the AI word meaning 'not what you'd expect'!), and I'm among them. If you think about it a while you'll see what it means, though. If not, well it's not *too* much of a handicap! The confusion arises because of the way the meaning of '=>' is bound up with how it's used to deduce new facts, which we will be coming across in the next section.

Finally, a look at '≡':

Bimbo has a tail ≡ Bimbo is a dog is ***true***
Bimbo has a tail ≡ Bimbo is not a dog is ***false***
Bimbo is not a dog ≡ Bimbo has a tail is ***false***
Bimbo hasn't a tail ≡ Bimbo is not a dog is ***true***

Right, I think we've just about exhausted that! If you don't know what the sentential connectives are by now, after those informal 'truth tables' which gave you the output for every combination of true and false inputs then you may have a little trouble with the rest of this book. It is really easier than it looks! Only the '=>' is slightly odd, and most people can ignore it until they need to think about it again.

So now we have ways to define propositions (you just state them) and to define combinations of propositions (using the sentential connectives). These combinations are called *sentences*. The connectives themselves can be defined in sentences made up of the other connectives so that, for example, all of the following are true:

$(P \equiv Q) \equiv (P \wedge Q) \vee ({\sim}P \wedge {\sim}Q)$

$(P \vee Q) \equiv ({\sim}P \wedge {\sim}Q)$

$(P => Q) \equiv (Q \vee {\sim}P)$

As an example of how to 'read' these, the first one says that $P \equiv Q$ is true if either P and Q are both true, or P and Q are both false (otherwise $P \equiv Q$ is false).

A sentence which is always true is called a *tautology* while one which is always false is a *fallacy* or *contradiction*. Ones which depend on the values of the Ps and Qs are neither (for example, '$P \wedge Q$' is a sentence, but it depends on what P and Q are as to whether it's a contradiction or not).

4.1 INFERENCE RULES

The discussion in the previous section of how to construct propositions, then, gives us the basis of the Propositional Calculus. One thing remains, however, namely how do we create new sentences from the old ones? If we have a set of initial facts (*axioms*), how can we deduce any new facts from these? We need to use what are called *rules of inference* (or *inference rules*), which allow us to build new sentences from our set of initial propositions and existing sentences. The most important of these is called *modus ponens*, or the '=> – elimination' rule. *Modus ponens*, or, more correctly, *modus ponendo ponens* is Latin for 'the mood that affirms'. What this says is that if you have two sentences which are both true, and one is of the form 'P' and the other is of the form 'P=>Q', then you can conclude that 'Q' is also true. So if I state:

Bimbo is a dog => Bimbo has a tail

then I only need give the proposition 'Bimbo is a dog' and the consequence of 'Bimbo has a tail' follows automatically. You can only apply the rule when the 'P' part of the 'P=>Q' is true. So although (Bimbo is not a dog => Bimbo is a dog) is true as a whole (due to the weird definition of the truth of a sentence using '=>'), you can't apply it unless 'Bimbo is not a dog' is true, too; and if it were, then presumably 'Bimbo is a dog' would be false (if they're defined to be the negation of each other), which would make the implication as a whole false and would also therefore stop you from making the inference. What I'm trying to give you here is an informal paraphrase of a formal definition of what you do informally all the time! So, if you don't follow what's going on, just look on modus ponens as meaning 'if I say that P implies Q is true, and that P is true, then I know that Q must also be true', and you won't go far wrong.

Why is it called '=> – elimination'? Simply because if both 'P' and 'P=>Q' were entries in some massive database, this inference rule would mean you could replace them both by 'Q', eliminating the sentential connective, '=>'. There's normally a pair of rules for each sentential connective, one which eliminates it and one which introduces it. The '=> – elimination' rule is the only one I'll talk about because it's the one which people know best of all. You can, incidentally, express the modus ponens rule as:

(P ∧ (P=>Q)) => Q

but you might think it's a bit suspicious to allow that since it needs the modus ponens rule – ie. itself – in order to be applied. It's all above board, though, trust me!

That, then, is the Propositional Calculus. A propositional logic like this isn't of much use to people in AI except for making it easier for them to understand the Predicate Calculus. This is because, typically, AI folk want to talk not only about whether propositions are true or false, but also about 'objects', ie. individual entities. There's no way in the Propositional Calculus of referencing, for example, 'player no. 17', 'the object inside this box', 'the number 142857', 'Albert Einstein' or 'this piece of cheese'. If you can't talk about objects, you can't talk about classifications of objects, or generalisations of the relationships between them. In order to do this, you need to use the Predicate Calculus.

4.2 THE PREDICATE CALCULUS

In the Predicate Calculus, we extend what we have already in the Propositional Calculus. The sentential connectives have the same meanings, but the logic is used in a different way. Rather than look at sentences merely because of their truth value, the Predicate Calculus comes in when you want to talk about specific objects – 'individuals' in the language of the logician. Normally, these individuals represent what you'd expect to be an object in the real world, maybe something you could pick up or bump into ('Elizabeth', 'Paddington Station', 'the wicked witch of the west'), or at least things you regularly talk about ('twenty-two', 'the charm quark', 'my database file'). There are cases where you can talk about other things, such as 'the rule that if it's raining and I haven't an umbrella and I'm outside then I'll get wet', but for the moment we'll ignore these.

If the Propositional Calculus is made up mainly of propositions, it's fair enough to suppose that the Predicate Calculus is made up mainly of predicates. So what's a predicate? A predicate is a statement about an individual, or about the relationship between individuals. It is a bit like a 'boolean function' in a conventional programming language, in that it takes a set number of 'arguments' and has a value of true or false depending on what arguments you gave it. So if you had a predicate 'edible' and applied it in turn to the individuals 'Tuesday', 'this toffee', 'yellow paint' and 'the gingerbread house' you'd get *false*, *true*, *false* and *true* respectively. The predicate 'sticky' would return *false*, *true*, *true* and *false* when applied to them in order (the last one would be true if *I* had made the gingerbread!). Other off-the-cuff examples of predicates are 'resides in Calcutta', 'made of carbon', 'is yellow' and 'is a subatomic particle'.

Predicates with more than one argument include things like 'is longer than', 'is next to' and 'is a kind of' (which have two arguments), and 'has factors of', 'primary colour with respect to' and 'in between' (which have three arguments). If you give a predicate with no arguments then it works just like a proposition in the Propositional Calculus (which isn't too surprising).

So how do you write these things down? Take a look at this list of a few true predicates:

```
holds(bag1, rat23)
hungry(tiger)
is_sum_of(14, 6, 8)
has_sides_of_length(polygon77, 19, 1, 3, 11)
door_open
```

Here, the predicates have been applied to certain arguments. I've just told you they're true – they could well be false in 'real life' – but, as is the case with the Propositional Calculus, statements which are made have a meaning independent to that which they enjoy in the world in general. If I made the assertion `striped(moon)` then it would still be true, even though the moon isn't actually striped in the physical universe. The words are only names, after all: if all occurrences of a word, such as `elephant`, were replaced by another word, say `omnibus`, then the logic system would be identical, and behave exactly the same as before (assuming that the name `omnibus` wasn't already in use!). This notion is called 'referential transparency', if you're interested. It would just be that much more awkward for a human observer to understand it if you gave things random names, similar to giving variables stupid identifiers in a program (for example writing a function `remove_element (OvalWindsweptCreams)` instead of `remove_element(Set)`).

4.3 THE UNIVERSAL QUANTIFIER

All the single-argument predicates can be used to define 'sets' of objects. To do this you take any one-place predicate, P, and apply it to all individuals. These individuals can then be split into two groups, those for which P(X) (where X is the individual) is true, and those for which it isn't. If P(X) is true, X is said to 'satisfy' P. So objects satisfy predicates. You can have subsets, of course, for example all the objects which satisfy 'bible(X)' will satisfy 'book(X)', therefore 'bible' is a subset of 'book'.

We can now say some quite powerful things; an assertion like:

```
has_axe(norbert) => dangerous(norbert)
```

enables us to add new predicates about individuals from old ones, by using modus ponens. However, what if there were several things which were dangerous if they had the axe? Apart from Norbert, maybe Karen and Maureen are dangerous with axes, too? That's easy, you just add:

```
has_axe(karen) => dangerous(karen)
has_axe(maureen) => dangerous(maureen)
```

Simple enough? But what about Esther, Harold, Walter, Jemima, Hans, LeRoy and so on? What you *really* want to say is that 'anything that has an axe is dangerous'. You do this using what's called the *universal quantifier*, the symbol for which is ∀, an upside-down 'A'. So to represent `anything that has an axe is dangerous` you'd use:

```
∀X. has_axe(X) => dangerous(X)
```

and that does the trick. ∀ reads as 'for all values of', so the whole of the above can be looked on as a shorthand for the vaguely English sentence, 'for all values of X, if X has an axe then X is dangerous'.

You can make these things arbitrarily complex. What if I said 'oh, but the definition given here means that if a tooth brush had an axe it would be dangerous.'? Easy enough to restrict it to people, it's just:

```
∀X. has_axe(X) ∧ person(X) => dangerous(X)
```

What about something with more than one variable, eh? How about 'for all objects X and Y, if X is adjacent to Y then Y is adjacent to X'? Well that's just:

```
∀X Y. adjacent(X, Y) => adjacent(Y, X)
```

You'll notice I'm using little letters for everything here except the 'variables' which are introduced by the quantifier, and I've put those in upper case. The things in little letters are either predicate names, or 'constants'. There's no reason why a constant shouldn't have the same name as a predicate, but connecting the two means you need 'meta-level' second-order operators, which I've not talked about yet! Sometimes people will use upper/lower case letters the other way round, I've picked this alternative because it's the way the AI language PROLOG does it. PROLOG has become a favourite among AI people over recent years, and is actually based on the Predicate Calculus. This makes it particularly useful in writing applications for which the Predicate Calculus is appropriate. It has some differences, the main ones arising because PROLOG is a language which is used to *run* a program, not merely a way of describing things. I'll continue to draw parallels between the Predicate Calculus and PROLOG for the remaining sections on KR, but I shan't go into the language itself in any detail.

Anyway, you can be as complicated as you like with this kind of thing. The expression:

```
∀X. large(X) => (∀Y. small(Y) => larger(X, Y))
```

means 'for all values of X, if X is large then for all values of Y, if Y is small, then X is larger than Y'. It is exactly the same as saying:

```
∀X Y. large(X) ∧ small(Y) => larger(X, Y)
```

4.4 THE EXISTENTIAL QUANTIFIER

There is another useful quantifier, the *existential quantifier*. This one has the symbol ∃, a backwards E, and is pronounced 'there exists'. So if I wanted to say 'there is a person who eats bicycles' I'd use:

```
∃X. person(X) ∧ eats_bicycles(X)
```

which reads 'there exists an X such that X is a person and X eats bicycles'. It doesn't mean there's *only* one person who eats bicycles, just that there's at least one. Here are some more examples of quantification and their English paraphrases:

```
∃X Y. dislikes(X, Y)
```
There exist an X and a Y such that X dislikes Y.

```
∃X. fallen_in_sea(X) => drowning(X)
```
There exists an X such that if X has fallen in the sea then X is drowning.

```
∀X. person(X) => ∃Y. person(Y) ∧ loves(X, Y)
```
For all values of X, if X is a person then there exists a Y such that Y is a person and X loves Y, or – more poetically – everyone loves someone!

As with the case for sentential connectives, quantifiers have inference rules. Unlike the case for sentential connectives, they don't have snazzy latin names! The '∀ – elimination' rule, for example, is called 'universal specialisation', and it says that if we have some expression E which mentions (among other things) the variable X, then if we also have:

```
∀X. E(X)
```

we can deduce E(I) for any individual I. So given that:

```
∀X. eats_meat(X) => carnivore(X)
```

we can use universal specialisation on any individual, Rodney, say, to get:

```
eats_meat(rodney) => carnivore(rodney)
```

without the ∀, you'll note. We can then look to see if Rodney eats meat, and, if he does, we can apply modus ponens and deduce that he's therefore a carnivore. See? It all hangs together! The universal specification rule is quite frequently used by people in conjunction with modus ponens. So much so, in fact, that folk expect it to be part of the definition of =>. So that's why =>'s formal definition looks wrong, we intuitively think of its use only in cases where the left-hand side is true, ie. whether it's 'applicable' or not. So if we see 'Bimbo is not a dog => Bimbo hasn't got a tail', we automatically assume that it means only dogs have tails, which can easily be wrong if Polly the parrot has one, too. However, since Bimbo *is* a dog, we can't make the inference anyway. If Bimbo weren't a dog, then he couldn't have a tail; hence, if he were a parrot he couldn't have one.

This is because the '=>' *says* he can't have one, if you want him to be able to have a tail then you have to change your rule. The '=>' can't help it if it doesn't match up with the real world! It's only false if the implication would make facts inconsistent, ie. if a true fact implies the negation of something which we already know is false, then the '=>' as a whole is false.

If you add to the Propositional Calculus the notions of predicates, quantifiers and quantifier inference rules, you get the full Predicate Calculus. Normally, people use a slightly adapted version which isn't any more powerful, just lets you say a few things more easily. This adaptation includes the notion of functions, and the predicate 'equal'. Functions are like predicates but they can return answers other than true or false. Something like 'add' is a function, as `add(2, 3)` returns 5, not true or false. Really, of course, it's just short for saying `add(2, 3, 5)` which reads 'add 2 to 3 and you get 5', and is how you'd put it in 'pure' PROLOG. The 'equal' predicate says that two individuals I and J are equal if, for all predicates P and functions F, P(I) ≡ P(J) and F(I) = F(J). These alterations mean that we don't have straight, unadulterated Predicate Calculus any more, we have something that's a 'first order logic'. Hmm, yet *more* names for you to take in!

What does 'first order' mean? It means that when you quantify, using either ∀ or ∃, you only do it over objects. You can't quantify over predicates, for example, as that would be second order. You can't quantify over quantifiers, either. So taking these one at a time:

```
∀X. ∃Y. knows(X, Y)
```

is first order,

```
∀X. ∃P. P(X)
```

is second order, and

```
∀Q. QY. big(Y)
```

is obscene! Second order predicates can be 'built' from first order ones, by having something like:

```
∀P X. truethat(P, X)
```

but this is a bit clumsy. You can also use a second order formalism to say things like:

```
plus(2, 7, 9)
reflexive(plus)
∀P X Y Z. reflexive(P) => P(X, Y, Z)≡P(Y, X, Z)
```

to describe the fact that `plus(X, Y, Z)` is the same as `plus(Y, X, Z)`, and you may have noticed I used second order informally when I defined 'equals' just now!

The theory is that the First Order Predicate Calculus provides you with all you ever need in a logic, and that any other logics can be formulated in first order terms if you like. This doesn't stop people designing logics of their own, of course, because for any application you tend to need specialised constructs, and these may be clumsy to state at brass tacks level. There's a preponderance of new logics in AI, however, and anyone claiming to be doing a formalisation of some technique invariably adds to the total.

The First Order Predicate Calculus does have a lot going for it, however. It's very simple, quite elegant, and if it doesn't make some complicated things *easy* to do, at least they're *possible*. It's also simple to prove things which are written in the language, and many automatic theorem-prover programs have been written which purport to do just that (with varying levels of success – they're often far too slow). If your own, home-grown logic can be translated into the first order Predicate Calculus quite easily, or, better still, if it's just a case of giving it a more powerful syntax, then you will also be able to draw on these advantages.

Even if you don't use the First Order Predicate Calculus, it's still easier by far to prove things if you stay at the first order level of whatever calculus you decide to use instead. In general, though, there's no difference so far as the computer is concerned which level of knowledge representation to use, they're all as easy as each other to store internally. Processing first order logics is much easier, however, although it can involve handling a lot of little steps which soon add up.

In AI applications, people almost invariably use either First Order Predicate Calculus (which I'll henceforth tend to abbreviate as FOPC), or they use First Order Logic (FOL). I'll talk about FOPC mainly, but if I do slip into FOL from time to time, at least now you'll know the difference! FOPC is a subset of FOL, in fact.

4.5 APPLICATIONS OF FIRST ORDER PREDICATE CALCULUS

It's no use my spending all this time telling you about FOPC without its having some relevance to computer games, and to MUDS especially. So how do you 'use' it in earnest, then? How can you employ it to describe something in an adventure game? Or in anything for that matter?

Well I'll try to show you by talking through an example. Let's make it simple, otherwise we'll be bogged down in the intricate details of what it is we're describing, when really I just want to get over the salient points involved in using the Predicate Calculus.

Suppose we're in a room with three objects: a crossbow, a crossbow bolt (or 'quarrel'), and a werewolf. The werewolf won't let us leave while it lives, and the only way to kill it is by shooting it with the crossbow. Assume this is part of a larger system, and there may be other objects around. If this is so, we have to make our formalisation general, so that it can work just as well if we had two quarrels in the room instead of one, say. Now how can we describe this situation in the FOPC?

Well we have three objects, let's give them names. So as to be nice and abstract, we'll call them `obj1`, `obj2` and `obj3`. These represent, respectively, the crossbow, the quarrel, and the werewolf. So our first three predicates (statements) are:

```
crossbow(obj1)
quarrel(obj2)
werewolf(obj3)
```

Now what actions do we wish to have? Well we need to be able to load the crossbow with the quarrel, and to kill the werewolf by discharging a loaded crossbow at it. We also need to be able to leave the room if the werewolf is dead. So we'll need some way of being able to tell when we can do, or have done, these actions.

Let's make it so that once we've loaded the crossbow with the quarrel, by using an action we'll call '`load`', we get:

```
loaded(obj1, obj2)
```

true, and:

```
unloaded(obj1)
```

false. Never mind how we manage that yet, we're just looking for ways to tell us the effects of the actions we've carried out so far. We'll also need the notions of:

```
alive(obj3)
```

and

```
dead(obj3)
```

for the other two actions, '`shoot`' and '`leave`'. If you felt like it, you could make `dead(obj3)` follow on from `~alive(obj3)`, but it's cleaner this way, although it needs more work. So we have four new predicates, two of which we can use to describe the initial state of the world, that is:

```
unloaded(obj1)
alive(obj3)
```

Now, however, we have a problem. If we started off with these two predicates, once we'd loaded the crossbow we'd want to retract the first one, ie. `unloaded(obj1)`, and assert `loaded(obj1, obj2)` (which means 'objl – the crossbow – is loaded with obj2 – the quarrel'). Similarly, once we'd killed the werewolf we'd like to get rid of `alive(obj3)` and replace it with `dead(obj3)` instead. But there's no way of *doing* that in the Predicate Calculus! Once you've said `alive(obj3)`, it's thereafter always true, for ever more, within your logic system. Adding `~alive(obj3)` gives you a contradiction, it doesn't supersede the earlier assertion at all. How do we get out of this?

4.6 STATES

What's needed is the notion of a *state*. Conceptually, a state is what the world looks like at a particular instant in time – a 'snapshot' if you like (or frame in the earlier film analogy). You could think of a state as being a description of 'what is true about the world at a certain moment in time'. An action which is executed in one state produces a new state which looks exactly the same as the first, except it's updated by the effects of the action. So a state is what the world model is like after executing an action, and an action behaves like a function which takes one state and produces another (a 'state-to-state function' in the textbooks, as I mentioned earlier). States are sometimes called 'situations'.

The easy way to represent states in the Predicate Calculus is quite simple: you just give them a name, maybe '`s1`' or something, and then adjust your predicates so that they're like:

```
unloaded(obj1, s1)
alive(obj3, s1)
```

instead of just having the one parameter. The new meaning of this second predicate, for example, is equivalent to 'obj3 is alive in state s1', or, if you prefer, 'obj3 is alive at time s1' (but not necessarily at any other times, of course). So states are really devices which let you say what the world is like after executing actions (ie. in between them). The solution can be complicated if several actions are trying to go on at the same time, as in MUDS, but the basic idea is still perfectly OK.

Things which are always true, such as the fact that obj2 is always a quarrel, you needn't bother adjusting to incorporate a state parameter. Alternatively, if you want to be *really* pedantic, you may prefer to use a 'consistent' notation and say something akin to:

```
∀S. crossbow(obj1, S)
```

I shan't bother with that here, though.

Let's look at our description of the world so far:

```
crossbow(obj1)
quarrel(obj2)
werewolf(obj3)
unloaded(obj1, s1)
alive(obj3, s1)
```

4.7 OPERATORS

So now we have our 'static' predicates, which cannot change, and our new 'dynamic ones' which can have different values depending on what states they exist in. Now we have to define the actions (or *operators*, as they are more properly termed) which get us from one state to another.

To load an object with another object, the first had better be an unloaded crossbow and the second had better be a quarrel. If not, we can't do anything along the lines of loading it. So let's define these preconditions to start with:

```
∀O I S. load(O, I, S) ≡
                        crossbow(O) ∧
                        unloaded(O) ∧
                        quarrel(I) ∧
                        (∃ C. loaded(C, I)) . . .
```

The '. . .' is because we've not finished it yet, these are just a few tests to make sure we'll be able to load the crossbow without messing up the universe. As it turns out, only crossbows can be unloaded anyway, so we can drop the first term if we like, it follows from the second. The last line, incidentally, says that the quarrel must not be loaded in any other crossbow ('there does not exist an object, C, such that C is loaded with I'). `O` stands for 'object', `I` for 'instrument' and `S` for 'state', by the way.

What do we want 'load' to do? Well we want it to produce a new state where the crossbow is loaded with the quarrel. We'll need to conjure up the name of this new state, '`Snew`', from somewhere, so we can do it either by putting '`∀ Snew.`' just before where we need it, or we can add another argument to the definition of 'load'. Although I've not done it here, it is, incidentally, common practice to 'assume' that all free variables are universally quantified anyway, to save the bother of writing '`∀`' in front of them all. This is a feature of PROLOG, for example. We don't *really* need to make `Snew` a parameter of 'load', but I shall do because it then allows us to ask questions about the past, such as 'could I have loaded the crossbow in state s4 and got state s5?', rather than just 'could I have loaded the crossbow in state s4'. Not *too* much of a difference, I admit, but it's also more PROLOG-like, and PROLOG is an AI language which is becoming increasingly popular, especially since it was chosen by the Japanese for their fifth generation computer project. I have other ulterior motives for making `Snew` a parameter, of course, namely that it's easier to discard when it's in this form than it is when it's not. This crops up in 'planning' programs, which I talk about later.

So back to our definition of `load` with its brand new parameter, which, when we include it, makes the predicate define `load(O, I, S, Snew)`. If we're using this new state, we ought to say that it's the one which follows the old one, so another precondition of load is:

```
follows(Snew, S)
```

What is true in `Snew`? Well, the crossbow is loaded with the quarrel, it is no longer unloaded, and all the other facts which were true in state `S` carry on in state `Snew` unaltered. Here we hit another obstacle: how do you say 'everything which was true in S is true in Snew' without resorting to use of the Second Order Predicate Calculus? Well with a larger number of state-dependent predicates we'd virtually *have* to use something like:

```
∀P. P(S) => O(Snew)
```

(adjusted for the appropriate number of parameters of the `Ps`), otherwise we'd spend all our lives typing them all in. Since we only have:

```
alive, dead, loaded, unloaded
```

though, we can list them all without too much hassle. To make things easier, we'll have a predicate called 'same' which tells us all that's the same from one state to another, assuming no changes at all were made. We know static, non state-dependent predicates like 'crossbow' and 'quarrel' (and now 'follows') are going to be OK anyway, so no need to mention them. For the rest, we define:

```
∀P1 P2 C1 B C2 S Snew. same(P1, P2, C1, B, C2, S, Snew)
≡
   (dead(P1, S) => dead(P1, Snew)) ∧
   (alive(P2, S) => alive(P2, Snew)) ∧
   (loaded(C1, B, S) => loaded(C1, B, Snew)) ∧
   (unloaded(C2, S) => unloaded(C2, Snew))
```

This makes it easier to list the effects of load, and we can now almost say it in its entirety. First, however, just a little definition which is pretty obvious but I ought to state it for the purists' peace of mind:

```
(A≠B) ≡ (A=B)
```

Right, now we can at last complete the final definition of load in the FOPC:

```
∀ O I S Snew. load(O, I, S, Snew) ≡
(crossbow(O) ∧
unloaded(O, S) ∧
quarrel(I) ∧
follows(Snew, S) ∧
(∃C. loaded(C, I, S))) =>
loaded(O, I, Snew) ∧
∀ P1 P2 C1 B C2. C2≠O =>
same(P1, P2, C1, B, C2, S, Snew)
```

and wasn't *that* a lot of work? Still, in English, it says:

> *For all values of O, I, S and Snew, loading O with I in state S to get Snew is the same as saying that if O is a crossbow which is unloaded in state S, and I is a quarrel, and state Snew follows on from state S, and there does not exist an object C such that C is loaded with O, then O will be loaded with I in the state Snew and everything which was true in state S is the same in state Snew except for ones involving the predicate for unloaded (ie. the parameter C2) if that parameter C2 is the object O which we loaded*

What a mouthful! It's much wordier than the logical formulation. So no wonder people designed the Predicate Calculus – it's *far* more succinct, once you get the hang of it.

That's now defined the first part of the situation which I described earlier. I'll just produce the definitions of the other two actions out of thin air and you can either work your way through them or ignore them:

```
∀O I S Snew. shoot(O, I, S, Snew) ≡
(werewolf(O) ∧
crossbow(I) ∧
follows(Snew, S) ∧
∃B1. loaded(I, B1, S)) =>
unloaded(I, Snew) ∧
dead(O, Snew) ∧
∀P1 P2 C1 B C2. (P2≠O ∧ C1≠I) =>
same(P1, P2, C1, B, C2, S, Snew)
∀S Snew. leave(S, Snew) ≡
(follows(Snew, S) ∧
(∃W. werewolf(W) ∧ alive(W
∀P1 P2 C1 B C2. same(P1, P2, C1, B, C2, S, Snew)
```

This second one is a bit redundant, since it doesn't make any changes to the world; if it did, they'd go after the `=>`. In common with the other actions, it doesn't actually use the predicate '`dead`', so we could get rid of it. I've kept it to balance '`alive`', so that they're mutually exclusive, although as I said earlier, negating '`alive`' would do just as well.

4.8 VARIATIONS ON A THEME

What I've presented to you, then, is the full Predicate Calculus. The FOPC forms the basis of most of the KR stuff that crops up in the remainder of this book. Although it is a complete, formal logic, the FOPC has several verbose and annoying features which you either don't need in most cases or which really go without saying. If you know the kind of thing you wish to talk about, then in that context some of the cumbersome ways of describing things in their complete, fully-detailed, explicit form can be down right irritating! These can be alleviated by minor changes to the syntax ('syntax' meaning the symbols you use – the words, order and shorthand for them), which overcome the problems if you know pretty well the standard, repeated kind of things your application is likely to need. They do, however, retain the flavour of the FOPC and, although I shan't be bothering you with the proofs here, can be shown to be equivalent in every way with the FOPC proper. The next sections, then, take a look at some of the ways in which the FOPC can be made more friendly, by the use of syntactic 'conventions' to save the time and effort of saying everything in its entirity. Any logic system which has the same facilities as some more basic system, but has a neater way of saying a few of the things which crop up a lot in their particular application, is said to be 'syntactically sugared'. So I'll presently be showing you some of the syntactically sugared versions of the FOPC.

Of course, if you use one of these tuned-up varieties of the FOPC to make it easier to say some of the things you commonly want to say, it follows that some of the things you don't often want to say may well be difficult to say, or even perhaps impossible, in this customised system. It's as if you usually have to 'pay' for the fact that some things are easier by some of them being more obscure and baroque. Hence, if you have some fact you want to represent in your modified calculus, you'll probably tend to take the easy way of doing it rather than making things hard for yourself by doing it the 'non-approved' way. So your choice of calculus restricts, in some sense, the choice of representations available to you, while at the same time increasing your expressive power by making some things easier to describe succinctly.

This may sound like a simple trade-off, but it's actually more complicated in that the language moulds your choice of representations by being so restrictive, and this can in fact *help* you at certain times. Take a simple sentence like 'the tree is tall'. How would you express this in the FOPC? Well here's a set of possibilities:

```
tree_is_tall
tall(tree)
height(tree, tall)
value(height, tree, tall)
```

Which do you use? Well it depends on your application. If you only have one object and it's a tree, then you never want to quantify over objects and you might as well forget them and just use the Propositional Calculus, which is the first case in this list. If you have several objects, and you want to talk about which ones are tall, then the second one will let you say '∀O. tall(O)'. But what if you wanted to describe all 3-dimensional objects, ie. ones which had a height (as opposed to a depth and a breadth, say)? You'd need to use the third case, where '∀O H. height(O, H)' would refer to all objects which had a height. Finally, what if you were required to talk about the properties of a particular object? 'Some property of the tree is that it is tall', say? Then you have to resort to the fourth case, and use '`∃P. value(P, tree, tall)`'.

Now if you use a syntactically sugared version of the FOPC you needn't bother about these issues, because one of them will generally be easier to use than all the others. To save you the burden of having to figure out the appropriate one every time, the particular dialect of the logic you are using will have 'built in' a natural way of doing it, consistent with everything else. For some simple applications, the straight, unadulterated Propositional Calculus may well do; in more complex ones, you might have to go for something more exotic.

So what *are* these variations on the FOPC theme, then? The next chapter describes a number of them, and where they're most useful. The ones we're interested in are those which are going to be most relevant to MUDS, since this is the object of the exercise, and because we need some good way of describing things in any MUD implementation (and hopefully one which beats the ad hoc ways used in existing adventure programs!).

5
PRACTICAL KNOWLEDGE REPRESENTATION

5.0 BINARY PREDICATES

The first variation of the FOPC which I shall discuss is a construct known as the *binary predicate*. The essential idea here is that you force all predicates which take more than two arguments to take only two, and introduce new predicates to cope with any extras. There are numerous advantages to this, which I'll outline later on, but one of them is that you can represent such predicates quite well graphically. This graphical representation is called a *Semantic Net* (or *Semantic Network*), and it makes the description of what's happening much easier to follow for the human being using it once they've learned how to read one.

The first problem, then, is how to devise this binary predicate system from the FOPC. Suppose we wanted to represent the fact '`Hilda kills the vampire with the stake`'. A reasonable representation of this, using the verb in the sentence as a predicate and the nouns as parameters to that predicate, might be:

```
kill(hilda, vampire, stake)
```

So we have a three-place predicate, `kill`, and three objects, `hilda`, `vampire` and `stake`.

The way to represent the same sentence using only binary predicates is to introduce a new object, a `killing`. Hilda may be especially chaotic in her philosophy of life, and may have killed several other evil beasties prior to doing over this vampire. We'll call each one of these events a `killing`. So we could rephrase the sentence to say 'there is a particular killing where Hilda is the killer, the vampire is the victim, and the stake is the weapon'. We could represent this as:

```
∃K. element-of(K, killings) ∧
    killer(K, hilda) ∧
    victim(K, vampire) ∧
    weapon(K, stake)
```

`Killings` is the name of a set of all the things we want to say are killings. We need it because in the natural way to put it, namely:

```
∃K. killing(K)
```

the predicate `killing` only has one argument, and we're after a set of two-argument functions. Hence the requirement for a longer way of putting it. So, we've got rid of one three-placed predicate and produced a set of four two-placed ones to replace it. Seems hardly worth the bother, does it? Well, we've not finished yet. Existential variables like `K` get in the way all the time, so we'll dispose of it by giving our particular killing a name of its own; we'll call it `killing1`.

In general you can get rid of any existential quantifier by either giving it a name, or, if it is within the body (*scope*) of a universal quantifier, by defining a *function* which relates the existential variable to the universal one. So let's say we had the expression:

```
∀P. person(P) ∧ ∃S. person(S) ∧ acquainted(P,S),
```

which reads 'for all Ps who are people there exists an S such that S is also a person and P is acquainted with S'. Suppose that the person with whom Ludwig is acquainted is Deborah. We could define a function `knowsF` which takes one parameter and returns the name of that person known by its parameter. So `knowsF(ludwig)` is `deborah`. Now we can throw away the existential quantifier ∃ and we get:

```
∀P. person(P) ∧ person(knowsF(P)) ∧
acquainted(P,knowsF(P))
```

This is syntactic sugar, an expression:

```
∀X. f(g(X))
```

is just a shorthand way of saying:

```
∀X. ∃Y. h(X, Y) ∧ f(Y)
```

and in our simple case `knowsF` and `acquainted` are almost identical, `knowsF` just returns the value which `acquainted` has as a second argument. In more complex examples it's not so vacuous as this, but since the examples *are* more complex they're harder to understand, too, so I decided to give one you might find easier to follow rather than one you'll baulk at. The function `knowsF` here, which is used to get rid of the ∃, is called a *skolem function*, and the process of getting rid of ∃s labours under the name of *skolemising* (it's not really necessary to remember that unless you develop a particular interest in it). If you just give the ∃ variable a name, as we did in the `killing1` case, then technically that's still skolemising, and `killing1` is a *skolem constant*. That means it's a function which returns one value all the time, and that value is the value of `K` which makes the whole expression true. As I said, it's shorthand.

Back to Hilda going wild with a stake, then. We now have a name for the killing event, `killing1`. To complete our binary predicate system, we must change all these predicates about the killing into functions referring to a particular killing. So we can make `killer(killing1, hilda)` into a function, `killerF`, where `killerF(killing1)=hilda`. This reads as 'the killer in killing1 is Hilda'. We'll use the predicate `equal` to compare the results of two functions. So we end up with:

```
element-of(killing1, killings) ∧
    equal(killerF(killing1), hilda) ∧
    equal(victimF(killing1), vampire) ∧
    equal(weaponF(killing1), stake)
```

This is now our final binary predicate form. But what good is it?

Well one thing which has come out of it is that although we've been inventing functions willy-nilly, the only predicates we're using are `equal` and `element-of`. We might want a third, `subset-of` which would be used for something like 'apple is a subset of fruit, and fruit is a subset of food, so apple is a subset of food', but in this particular example we can get away without it. Restricting things to just these three predicates makes it that much easier to decide how to represent new concepts in the system – you get to invent as many functions as you require, but can't use any extra predicates. That means you don't have to think so much when you want to stick in a new fact, you can split it up into binary predicates and use them, rather than mess about wondering whether to use a three-place, two-place, one-place or zero-place predicate for that particular individual fact.

5.1 BINARY PREDICATE MODULARITY

The controlled limitation of the number of predicates we're using is not a good enough reason in itself for using this logic system, however, it's almost a side effect rather than a design decision. What binary predicates really buy you is modularity. Indexing on events, such as `killing1`, in this manner means you can chop and change around your definitions with very little difficulty. So if we wanted to add to our original `kill` predicate a fourth argument, say the scene of the crime, we'd need to change it to, say:

```
kill(hilda, vampire, stake, cave)
```

This might have extensive repercussions elsewhere in the system, because at each point where we've referenced `kill` with three parameters, we now have to modify it to four, even though we don't necessarily want to use that parameter in the expression. No sooner have we added in all the location parameter, than we find we need to add a fifth (time) and then a sixth (witness). These changes will necessitate further alterations to the predicates we've already written. However, if we use the binary predicate regime, all our existing expressions in the logic remain unchanged, they only take two arguments and neither of them are affected by the addition of new facts. `WeaponF(killing1)=stake` is going to be true no matter what other facts you add about `killing1`. The only way to preserve previously defined predicates in the normal FOPC is to make it upward compatible by having two predicates which say virtually the same thing, for example, both:

```
kill(hilda, vampire, stake)
```

and

```
kill(hilda, vampire, stake, cave).
```

This is clearly a hack, and is going to be confusing in the long-run, especially when it comes to updating predicates in new states as the result of applying actions. It is necessary to update all the earlier-version predicates – those with fewer parameters – just to maintain the integrity of the older expressions which reference them!

5.2 SEMANTIC NETS

There are other ways to build on the idea of binary predicates, but I'll end with a word on Semantic Nets. These are graphical (yes, pictures) representations which can easily be run up from a collection of binary predicates. To illustrate this, here is a set of facts:

```
Hilda kills the vampire with the stake
Hilda is happy
The vampire is upset
Hilda is alive
The vampire is undead
```

and here is the associated collection of binary predicates:

```
element-of(killing1, killings) ∧
    equal(killerF(killing1), hilda) ∧
    equal(victimF(killing1), vampire) ∧
    equal(weaponF(killing1), stake)

element-of(feeling1, feelings) ∧
    equal(feelerF(feeling1), hilda) ∧
    equal(emotionF(feeling1), happy)

element-of(feeling2, feelings) ∧
    equal(feelerF(feeling2), vampire) ∧
    equal(emotionF(feeling2), upset)

element-of(existence1, existences) ∧
    equal(existerF(existence1), hilda) ∧
    equal(stateF(existence1), alive)

element-of(existence2, existences) ∧
    equal(existerF(existence2), vampire) ∧
    equal(stateF(existence2), undead).
```

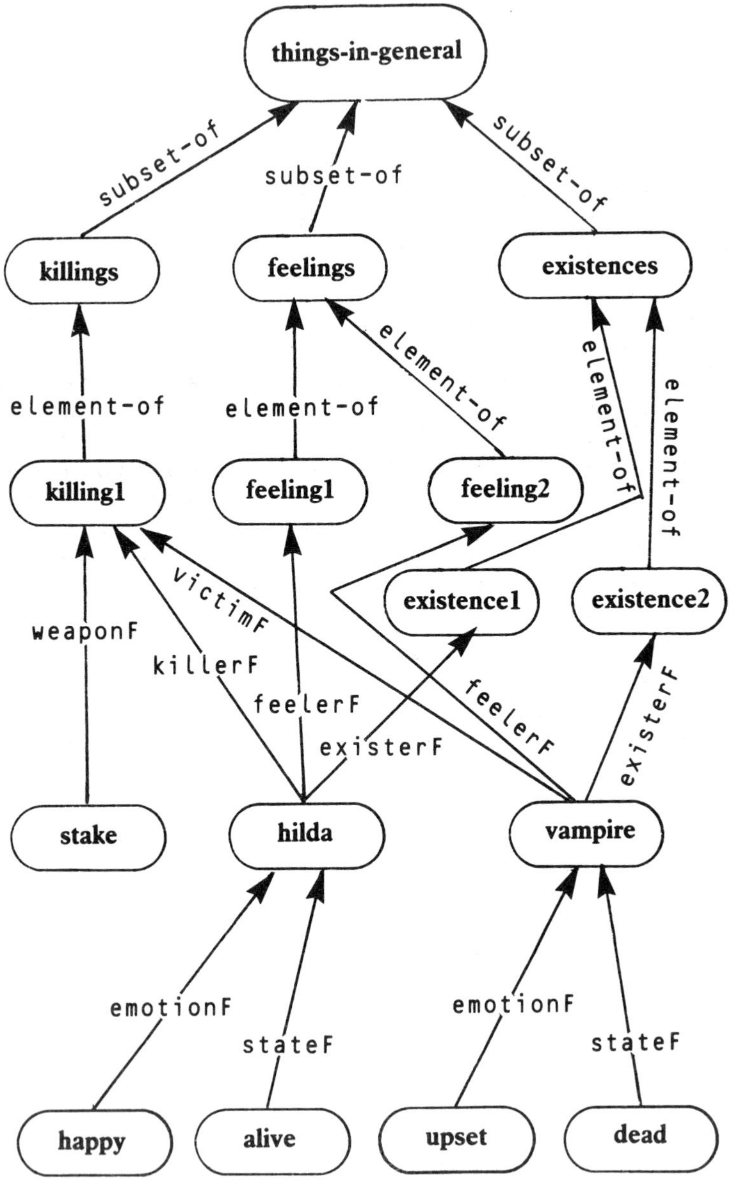

Figure 5.1 A semantic net

To represent this state of affairs as a Semantic Net is quite easy, you take all the objects (`hilda`, `vampire`, `stake`, `happy`, `upset`, `alive`, `undead`), the keys which index them (`killing1`, `feeling1`, `feeling2`, `existence1`, `existence2`) and the names of the sets to which they belong (`killings`, `feelings`, `existences`), and you write them all down in boxes. These will be the nodes of the network. The arcs connecting the nodes are arrowed lines, each bearing a label. The label is the name of the function or predicate which relates the two ideas. For example, with `element-of(killing1, killings)`, draw a line starting at the `killing1` box, ending with an arrowhead pointing at the `killings` box, and marked `element-of`. For `equals`, where the parameters are always going to be a function and the value with which its result is equal, say `equal(emotionF(feeling1), happy)`, draw a line from the first object, `feeling1`, to the second one, `happy`, and mark the arc with the function name, `emotionF`. If you had included a collection of subset relationships such as:

```
subset-of(killings, things-in-general)
subset-of(feelings, things-in-general)
subset-of(existences, things-in-general)
```

then you'd treat them like `element-of`, but labelling them `subset-of` instead.

If we were to express our set of sentences diagrammatically as a Semantic Net, by reading directly off the associated binary predicates (including the ones for `subset-of`), we would obtain the picture shown in Figure 5.1.

5.3 USES OF BINARY PREDICATES

So when would you use binary predicates rather than the normal FOPC? Well essentially, it's when you're doing 'development' work. It's quite a verbose way of writing things, but it guarantees that you can make sharp, short changes to the system without fear of interfering with the 'debugged' part you have already described. It also has the added plus of being easily drawn out in pictures (ie. Semantic Nets), which clarifies what you want to say. Once it has settled down, and the development is just about completed, you could then go back to the full FOPC and rewrite the system in that (or, better still, get a computer program to do it!).

This kind of adaptable knowledge structure is very desirable in adventure games. It means you can add new facts – objects, rooms, vehicles and so on – to your imaginary world, without affecting those facts which are already resident in it. And because everything is expressed in terms of only three predicates, when you do add a new fact you only have to ask yourself a few standard questions and you can define it: 'What is this fact an element of?'; 'What sets are this fact a subset of?'; 'What are the things about this fact which relate it to other facts?'.

This last question is the hardest to answer, because functions in binary predicates tend to relate specific kinds of objects together. For an event, like a `killing`, there will always be functions which define the primary objects involved. These in turn will have *properties*, which may in turn involve other objects. There's a loose structure to it all, and you might add several spurious assertions to the logic in the course of trying to describe a situation, while missing the important ones. That's OK because spurious ones don't do any harm, and if we *do* add new statements they don't foul up the ones we already have. So even if you do make a mistake, it's easy to remedy it.

So far I've only shown you how to represent straight facts in binary predicate logic. Representing actions is trickier. I shall, for the moment, ignore the question of actions and concentrate on representing pieces of information about objects. Having a special stylised calculus for handling actions is probably a good idea, and indeed that's what I'll talk of at some stage later on. For the moment, though, I'll stick to simple assertive sentences.

So we know what the binary predicate system is useful for, but it still seems a bit verbose. All the sentences break down into conjunctions of the same form: an `element-of` (or `subset-of`) definition, followed by a set of `equal` predicates, each comparing a function call (with the event as parameter) to an object. We can, of course, use the calculus to say other things: to compare the results of two functions, or to talk about function names as elements of sets and so on – although we haven't needed to so far. Whenever you have a set format for your data in a FOPC system, and it is annoyingly verbose to say it in full, the best way out is to create a new incarnation of the FOPC which takes out the verbosity and makes things easier to describe. We might not be able to compare the results of two functions any more, or to use predicates other than `element-of`, `subset-of` and `equals`, but then, they don't seem very necessary – so far – do they? The next section takes this idea a step further, and introduces the most popular, powerfully expressive knowledge representational system used in AI, the *Frame*, which is also, as it turns out, pretty useful for adventure games, too!

5.4 FRAMES

The first thing to point out about frames is that they have absolutely nothing to do with the Frame Problem mentioned earlier. 'Frame' here refers to a framework, a superstructure onto which you can add details, the equivalent of doors, roof, and bumpers being assembled to the frame of a car. Some of the things you add to the frame will have their own frames, like the engine, perhaps. *Why* it's this sort of frame should be apparent once I've described to you what one looks like.

If we analyse the structure of the binary predicates, we'll see they have the following form:

```
element-of(name, set) ∧
    equal(function1(name), object1) ∧
    equal(function2(name), object2) ∧
            ...
    equal(functionN(name), objectN)
```

We notice that `name` (eg. `killing1`) is on every line here so there's really no point in putting it in, we know it's going to be there anyway. Using some symbol `::`, say, and putting our `name` in front of it will give:

```
name :: ...
```

which means 'In the definition which follows, if I miss any parameters out of the functions then just put `name` there instead'. This is just a notational convenience, it doesn't alter *what* we say, it just shortens *how* we say it. It's like a textual macro, 'every time I say this, I really mean this'. The next thing to note is that on the line after we have a predicate, either `element-of` or `subset-of`. We could be more general here if we liked and allow any number of these. We'll keep them as they are, but let's drop the brackets, we *know* they're supposed to be there so there's no reason why we have to write them down all the time. The same goes for the ∧ symbols, it's always going to be a conjunction so we can just assume it. Finally, what about those `equals` that make up the rest of the lines which follow; we can forget them too, since they're always `equals` and never anything else.

Here is our `killing1` event in this new, lean language:

```
killing1::
    element-of : killings
    killer : hilda
```

```
victim : vampire
weapon : stake
```

And that's what is called a Frame! Yes, I know I dropped the '`F`' off the end of the function names – we know they're functions anyway so we might as well not bother telling ourselves. The above is exactly the same as the binary predicate representation, only it uses a different syntax/notation. The *meaning* (semantics) is the same, it just looks more concise. The '`:`' is used to separate out function and result, incidentally, so they look related to each other rather than just part of a column.

In AI terminology, we'd say that something like `killing1` is a 'Frame'. The function names, on the left-hand side of the `:`, are *slots*, and the results, to the right of the `:`, are the *values*. So we could, for example, say 'the value of the `weapon` slot of `killing1` is `stake`'.

Frames crop up everywhere in AI, and aren't always even called Frames! Other names used include *schema* and *units*. Frames is the older, and most widely-used term, however. Slots and values are pretty persistent, also common are *properties* instead of slots, and you will occasionally see *slotnames* and *slotvalues*.

The terms `element-of` and `subset-of` are not in general use, the preferred names are, respectively, `is-a` and `ako`. Since '`killing1` is an element of `killings`', it can be shortened by dropping either the `is an` bit of the connecting phrase or the `element of` part. In describing things from scratch, `element-of` is clearer, but we will use the more standard `is-a` form. `ako` means *a kind of*, so 'red is a subset of colours' could be equally well expressed as 'red is a kind of colour' – getting rid of the pluralisation of 'colour'. Since most work on Frames in AI uses the `ako` phraseology, henceforth I shall do, too.

Frames are best described as an organising principle. Once you start thinking about representing facts in an organised fashion, AI people use the term *knowledge* rather than just facts or assertions. This is just a sort of convention, but underlying it is a deep feeling that the key to knowledge lies in the way facts are organised. Knowledge is not the same as information, and things can be information without being knowledge. The way the universe handles unified field theory is a piece of information, but as no-one, not even the most expert physicist, knows how exactly the universe *does* do it, it's not yet knowledge. Knowledge is explicit, information may be implicit in the definition of things, and you may require some hypothesising to come up with an explicit theory of what implicit information describes.

Frames look far removed from the FOPC upon which they're based, but at least we can now talk in terms of them in the safe and sure knowledge that everything we're doing has a sound theoretical base. Frames are a relatively recent idea in AI (being invented around 1975), but have come to dominate several areas of the subject. This may surprise you, because at first glance they look just like records in PASCAL (and even, heaven forbid, in COBOL!). Just take a look, they have field names. OK so these are called slots but what does that matter? And these fields can have values. That's a record, then, isn't it? Well, yes, but the things we're going to do with Frames you'd be very hard-pressed to do with records! Being able to add new fields in the blink of an eye isn't the sort of thing you can expect of PASCAL records, although it would, of course, be possible in an interpretation of Frames in PASCAL, using some linked list structure. That's by the by, though, Frames are an *abstract* data type, independent of the language which is intended to use them.

5.5 EXPRESSIVE POWER OF FRAMES

What kind of power do Frames give us, then? Well suppose we were to try to represent a set of similar kinds of object such as, for a simple example, different kinds of citrus fruit. For our hypothesised application we need to consider their colour, their shape, which bits are edible and which bits aren't. We might have the following three Frames:

```
orange::
    ako : fruit
    colour : orange
    shape : round
    edible : inside
    inedible : outside

lemon::
    ako : fruit
    colour : yellow
    shape : oval
    edible : inside
    inedible : outside

banana::
    ako : fruit
    colour : yellow
```

```
        shape : long
        edible : inside
        inedible : outside
```

From this we can see that the information on which bits are edible and which bits aren't edible is identical for all the citrus fruit we are considering. So it will be easier if we can just say that anything which is a kind of fruit automatically inherits the properties of being edible inside and inedible outside? To do this we just add the fact to the Frame for `fruit`. This means that everything which is `ako` fruit inherits those slots and values. We might wish to override these default values for some other kinds of fruit (you can eat the outside of apples but not the very inside). To enable us to do this, we'll say that if something lower in the `ako` hierarchy has a slot defined for it with the same name as one higher up, then the lower one and its descendants don't take the value from the superclass (which in this example is `fruit`) but instead inherit from the more specific value (`apples`). OK, well if we want to include apples, our property-inheritance mechanism enables us to write:

```
fruit::
    ako : food
    edible : inside
    inedible : outside
    tastes : delicious

orange::
    ako : fruit
    colour : orange
    shape : round

lemon::
    ako : fruit
    colour : yellow
    shape : oval

banana::
    ako : fruit
    colour : yellow
    shape : long

apple::
    ako : fruit
    colour : green
```

```
shape : round
edible : outside
inedible : inside
```

Apples, then, are a kind of fruit but unlike the rest they are inedible inside and edible outside. They still taste delicious (a third property of fruit which I added). This inheritance mechanism can be either notational (just to save you the bother of writing down that something has a property shared by all elements of the same class), or deductive (there are implication rules which say 'if X has property P and Y is `ako` X then Y has property P'). I prefer the latter convention; after all, there *is* a limit to the number of things you can cram into a notation before it gets confusing!

Incidentally, noticing that both bananas and lemons were yellow in the above example, we could decide to have a class `yellowfruit` which had the inheritable property of being `yellow`. We might also see that both apples and oranges are round, and have another class `roundfruit` which is `ako` fruit, and all `roundfruit` have a `round` property. If we then introduced a new fruit which is both round *and* yellow, say a `grapefruit`, we would want it to be in *both* classes, and inherit the properties of both `yellowfruit` and `roundfruit`. This means that must allow Frames to have more than one `ako` slot, which is no problem. We also have to be careful not to inherit conflicting properties such as both 'edible inside' and 'inedible inside'. This can get quite complicated as you need to know which slots are mutually exclusive (eg. '`edible`' and '`inedible`') and which aren't (eg. '`edible`' and '`colour`').

If you want to make slots have more than one value, for example apples can be both red and green at the same time, you can either use two slots with the same name:

```
colour : red
colour : green
```

or you can have a list of values under one slot. Lists come in round brackets normally, so we could put:

```
colour : (red green)
```

This second way is marginally preferable in the Frame system as it is outlined here because, using the first form there is the problem that if apples, say, were `ako greenfruit` and inherited the colour green property, would the colour red property be in addition to it or would it override it? This second form always overrides, but then again you have to remember to add in the colour green, too, unless the inheritance is handled by some kind of inference mechanism which works it all out for you.

5.6 ADAPTATIONS OF FRAMES

Frames can be augmented in many ways. One way, used in Natural Language understanding, uses an adaptation called the *script*, which has as its slot values the names of other Frames which describe sub-events of a particular main event. The example usually shown is for the 'visiting a restaurant' script (Frame), where once you get in you use your 'attract the attention of the waiter' script, your 'select food' script, your 'eat food' script, either your 'compliments to the chef' or 'storm out in disgust' script (depending on the quality of the food) and your 'pay for meal' script. Each of these might refer to other scripts, or to primitive actions like 'devour food'. More about this later.

Scripts get their name because they look like scripts for plays, they form a sequence of events which need to be run through in order. They're more detailed of course, because the order can change (you could order the coffee before or after the sweet course, say). Also, they have references to sub-scripts, which are more detailed still.

Scripts are generally used for 'understanding' stories, and are operated by matching parts of the script against the story. So if the paragraph you wanted your program to understand started off 'I went to Strikes and ate a hamburger', it would recognise 'Strikes' as a restaurant and so take a look at the restaurant script. Seeing that the first two slots, (about attracting the attention of the waiter and selecting a menu) were missing, it would infer that they had occurred, and that nothing untoward had happened in the process.

Often, though, scripts are interesting because of what they fail to match. 'I went to the local burger bar and broke a tooth on a rusty screw' is still a restaurant script (unless you went to the burger bar deliberately to break a tooth!), but it falls down because something interesting and unexpected happened. The interest is precisely because the event is not in the script, so the script cannot therefore be expected to cover it. It needs to 'learn' from events, so that if something similar happens in the future, it can remember the previous occurrence ('This reminds me of the time I broke a tooth on a ball bearing in a fish and chip shop').

Scripts are now superseded by *Memory Organisation Packets* (MOPS), which are easier to use for learning, and are less susceptible to certain common script problems, such as interaction between simultaneously active scripts ('Edgar walked into the restaurant to ask directions for Covent Garden, and stayed to have lunch'), and the wrong scripts being considered ('I ran into the restaurant and caught my dog' is *not* a call to the restaurant script!). Since scripts and MOPS are basically Frames, though, I won't be giving them any special consideration in the remainder of this book.

Other things you can do with Frames include dangling bits of program off them. This is only for when you use Frames in some programming application. You might, for example, have a Frame to represent a company running a business. One of the Frame slots might be the annual turnover. If it was a large company, this might be difficult to calculate. So what you could do is just leave the method of calculation as the value part of the `turnover` slot. Then, if someone queries your knowledge base ('database' isn't quite the same thing – 'knowledge base' implies lots of structure) and asks for the turnover, you can run the small program you wrote to calculate it. If they don't, well that's fine, at least you didn't spend two hours working it out when you designed the system, only for it to be a wasted exercise.

Linking code to Frames is called *procedural attachment*, and was once quite fashionable but is not now as popular as it was. It is also difficult to justify in terms of the FOPC underlying the system. Using code to represent things is called *procedural knowledge*, whereas saying it all out in the open is *declarative knowledge*. Procedural is implicit, declarative is explicit. As knowledge could be taken to mean 'information about the universe which has always existed implicitly within the universe but which has now been made explicit', the concept of procedural knowledge unfortunately starts off on very shaky ground!

As I said, then, Frames are an organising device to make it easier for you to both represent facts/knowledge, and to partition the knowledge up into manageable chunks. The FOPC is free, wild, untamed, and you can say whatever you like in virtually any way you like. Therefore, things tend to be a bit haphazard when they're represented in it. Frames still provide a great deal of freedom, but they help the people who use them (knowledge engineers) to organise their ideas into a coherent form – one which is easy to change if needs be. The FOPC is predicate-oriented, whereas Frames put the emphasis on objects.

So Frames are very powerful. You can still draw Semantic Nets from them, as they're really just jumped-up binary predicates. Their main strength is the way they enable people to order their ideas into units of explicit information. Frames come in many shapes and forms, but the one I have just described is a reasonable conglomeration of the basic ideas. If Frames are that good, then, how could we go about representing some adventure – type knowledge in them?

5.7 THE WIZARD'S STUDY

The best way to show someone how to use something is by demonstration, so here is a discussion of how you'd represent a typical kind of room found in an adventure, a *Wizard's Study*. Before describing it, however, here are a few pcints about what I intend to do, to set your minds at rest.

Firstly, remember that Frames are an abstract way of representing knowledge. It doesn't matter how they're actually implemented, they still look the same when you write them down. Implementational matters don't, on the whole, matter here. *Some* do, of course, for example trying to keep in memory a representation of an entire city with fifty thousand inhabitants. Generally, though, it turns out that Frames are a rather economic way of storing information anyway, especially if you know in advance how much 'room' a particular kind of slot value is likely to need. If I said that a candle had a `burning` property of either true or false, and that its `contained by` property was room number 87, then that doesn't mean two slots are implemented to use the same amount of space, in fact they probably wouldn't be. Assuming you *were* worried about memory restrictions in your operating environment, you could patch `burning` into one bit if you wanted, and keep `contained by` wide enough for a whole address to point at the `room87` Frame. However, when writing them down it doesn't matter about this kind of thing because it is almost irrelevant *how* you implement Frames really, the important thing is whether you *can* or not! I've no intention of giving fragments of code to say how to represent Frames internally, because that's implementation-independent.

If you remember what I said some time ago about the difference between specification and implementation, and are worried about whether this Frames stuff (which is at the specificational end) is feasible at the implementational end, then don't be; Frames have been tried and tested in AI work, and they are in no way inefficient or clumsy when it comes to storing facts about objects!

The other point I'd like to make before I set off describing this Wizard's Study is that it's only going to be in terms of objects. If there are any actions which you might want to perform on the objects, these are not fully covered here. The reason is that I've not yet described in detail the format of actions, because in order to make them effective they have to be bundled up along with the Natural Language understanding part of the program, which is yet to be explained. Other things which are also more Natural Language oriented will crop up, too, for example adjectives are often properties of objects, and are only really needed to distinguish one object of a particular kind from another.

So let's represent this Wizard's room using Frames. We'll keep it fairly simple to make things easier, and thus ignore all spatial relationships except for inside/contains and on/under. To start with, then, we'd better have a couple of doors, with the second one hidden behind a bookcase. Make this second one a small door, to distinguish it from the first. On the bookcase we'll have some books, say *Libram of Incantations*, *Book of the Damned – Part 1*, *Book of the Damned – Part 2*, and *Tome of Tricks*. The *Tome of Tricks* has a bookmark in it.

Also in the room we'll have a table, for our wizard to work on, which supports a candle, a tinderbox and the wizard's trusty magic wand. Also, there's a chest for stationery, containing a quill pen, ink, and a papyrus scroll. On the opposite side of the room is a shelf, bearing numerous bottles containing potions of assorted colours: red, brown, and two green; and of varying sizes: small and large. Next to this we'll have a hatstand upon which the wizard has perched his conical hat, his staff, and his cloak. In the pouch of the cloak is a live frog, and a large, rusty key.

A fair enough description of a room! Now let's write it in terms of Frames.

5.8 HIERARCHY OF OBJECTS

The best place to start is by building up some kind of a hierarchy of object types, then we can use inheritance to the full. Really, it should be actions which determine the way we bundle up objects into classes (there's no point in sticking all objects with a similar property together if the property is never used!), but for the moment we'll assume that all properties are going to be relevant somewhere. Actions will still have some influence (what, after all, does the 'breakable' property say except that you can use the action 'break' on it?) but we'll try to keep them out of the way.

For inheritance purposes, it's probably a good idea if we don't try to bunch together things which are of the same type only because they share a common property, especially if it turns out that that property it likely to change when certain commands are given by the player.

So sticking a `stationery` label on all the stuff in the stationery chest and hoping to inherit the fact that their position is `inside chest` from the `stationery` Frame is unwise, as it only takes someone to come along and remove the object from the chest for it to no longer be in it, and therefore to get some 'interference' from the `stationery` class with regards to where its position should be. There are obvious ways this can be handled: for example, making the more specific, lower-level information win the duel. But I'll avoid the problem altogether by only using inheritance for properties which are never going to be changed (all the bottles are always made of glass, for example).

Let's start out by naming all our objects. Roughly in order of appearance in the room definition above, we have the following:

```
room - door1 - door2 - bookcase - libram - book1 -
book2 - tome - bookmark - table - candle - tinderbox -
wand - chest - quill - ink - scroll - shelf - bottle1 -
bottle2 - bottle3 - bottle4 - potion1 - potion2 -
potion3 - potion4 - hatstand - hat - staff - cloak -
frog - key
```

– thirty-two of them.

The natural groupings we get upon a cursory scan of these are:

```
doors
supports (table, bookcase, shelf, hatstand)
artefacts (wand, staff)
books
clothes
bottles
potions
everything left over
```

Let's take a look at these groupings and see if we can find anything else in common apart from their being roughly the same kind of thing:

Doors – what makes something a door is a combination of its shape (oblong), and the fact it's made out of wood. It has hinges, a handle and a keyhole, too, but we'll only keep the keyhole and forget about the others as they aren't really necessary (the keyhole wouldn't be either if we didn't have a key!).

Supports – what makes a support a support? Well they're all made of wood, but apart from that it's really a commonality of usage which binds them together, that is to say that they're all used for putting things on. When things are similar because of the way they are used, as supports are here, then it's a sure bet that there's an action involved somewhere along the line. Here it is the 'put object on support' action which leads us to think that these objects should be of the same type. So we'll leave a class `support` around for our imaginary command interpreter to utilise later on.

Artefacts – what is it about artefacts that makes us want to create a class for them? Again, it's primarily usage – you can zap things using artefacts! We'll be a little more conservative here, though, and just say that they have a property of being `magic`. They are also pole-shaped and made of wood.

Hang on, that's the third class of objects we've had which are made of wood. Might it not be a good idea to have a class of `wooden objects`, of which doors, supports and artefacts are sub-classes? Yes, not a bad move. Can we join up any of the other groups like that? Sure enough, we can – the tinderbox, chest and key are all metal objects, and the books, scroll and bookmark are all paper objects. There's no point in having `glassobject` as a class, because the only glass objects are bottles, so we might as well use `bottle` itself. We can go through all the objects like this, deciding what they're made of (useful if we ever want to write an `ignite` action!).

Potions – and what about the potions? And the ink? What are they made of? Considering what they're made of isn't really necessary here, because they're liquids, and what distinguishes liquids from each other in this world we are designing seems to be their colour. So we'll have something called a liquid (also useful if we decide to have a `drink` action). The rest of the things we have are solids. The major factor which separates solids from one another is what they are made of. For liquids, it's what colour they are.

The only other properties which don't change and which we might want to consider are size, weight and value. We'll combine the first two together, saying that in our simple world if something is of size `large` it is of weight `heavy`, and if it's of size `small` it's of weight `light`. No sense in cluttering it all up with notions of density at this point! We're now in a position to give a rough classification of the objects in a tree-like structure, with the parent/child relation of 'a kind of' (`ako`) – just right for Frames! This is done in Figure 5.2.

So far, what we have is a straight tree, as no nodes have more than one parent. We can make it more complex, by, for example, distinguishing between things which are breakable and things which

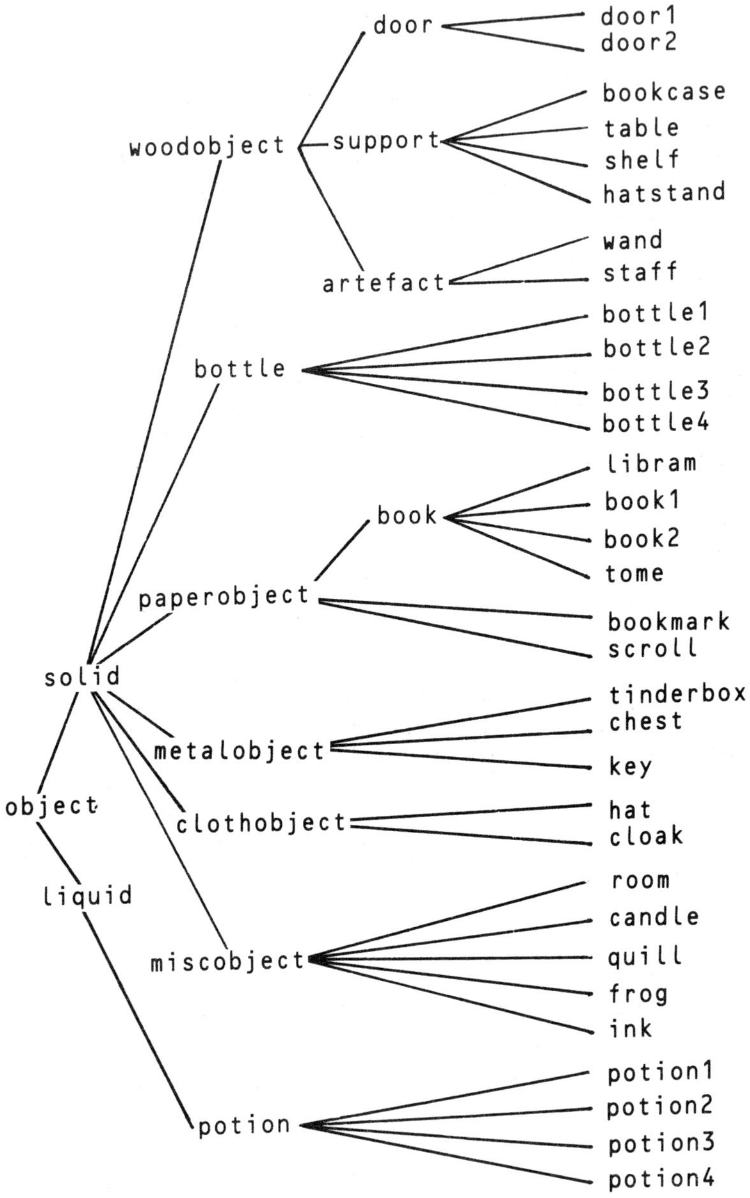

Figure 5.2 **Classification of Objects in the Wizard's Study.**

are not. Only solids can be breakable, and even then only wooden objects, bottles, candles and quills. We'd be able to slide this straight into the same tree because there's no 'conflict' involved, no objects are members of the class unless their siblings (ie. objects with the same parent) are also in the new class. The same thing would happen if we introduced a `tearable` class, to represent all the objects for which `tear` is a meaningful action; we'd have been able to build it into the tree simply by joining `paperobject` and `clothobject` together as children of a new class, `tearable`.

We can, however, complicate matters by introducing some *disjoint* classes. To make a new ako-hierarchy which exists simultaneously with this one, we need to have objects that have different parents in the original hierarchy but which have the same parent as each other in the new hierarchy. So let's introduce a class called `heavy-object`, which we use for all objects of size `large`. Now, we needn't state that an object is large when we give its frame, we only need to say that it is `ako heavyobject` and it will inherit the property. Similarly, we can have one for `lightobject`, of which all the light objects are members. Then, later on, we could arrange things so that if you tried to pick up something which was `ako heavyobject` it would give a sarcastic message or break your back or something. This way, the table and hatstand may be heavy, and the shelf and both the artefacts may be light. We can't say 'all supports are heavy' because they're not, and we can't join together the artefacts and the shelf as `lightobjects` and make this `ako` support, because the artefacts aren't supports. The new ideas of lightness and heaviness cut across the tree structure, and produce their own hierarchy of inter-related classes. So we may, in fact, have two or more valid hierarchies at the same time, if we allow nodes to have more than one parent. So long as there are no loops (no node is directly descended from itself), this will be fine.

5.9 THE WIZARD'S STUDY IN FRAMES

Enough description, now let's see if we can write some of this down as frames. I won't do it all, though, because there are thirty-two individual objects here and although it's not too hard to list them in frame form, they would take up too much space.

We'll start with the class of objects. From here we can hang all our default values. In our Wizard's Room, we don't have any inheritable slots which can have more than one value, except for `ako` and relations like `contains` and `on top of`. So there's no need to bother with deciding what to do if an inheritable slot is over-ridden lower down in the tree, it acts as a simple superseding of the more general inheritance. In addition, we never inherit conflicting values for slots from different, unrelated ancestors in the hierarchy (which might cause problems). I specially constructed the world this way, of course, and it's quite clean as a result. See what I mean about the language making it easy to represent things in good ways and harder in bad ones? So, here are the frames, preceded by short explanatory comments.

Objects are worth nothing, by default. Objects aren't ako anything, they're at the root of the ako hierarchy:

```
Object::
    worth : nothing
```

Heavy objects are a kind of object, ones whose size is large:

```
heavyobject::
    ako : object
    size : large
```

Light objects are a kind of object, those with a small size:

```
lightobject::
    ako : object
    size : small
```

Wooden objects are a kind of object, and are made of wood:

```
woodobject::
    ako : object
    made-of : wood
```

Doors are a kind of wooden object, oblong in shape, and they have a keyhole built in:

```
door::
    ako : woodobject
    shape : oblong
    built-in : keyhole
```

Door1 is ako door, and also ako heavy object:

```
door1::
    ako : door
    ako : heavyobject
```

Door2 is ako door, and is also a light object:

```
door2::
    ako : door
    ako : lightobject
```

Artefacts are wooden objects which are magical and shaped like poles. Their default value is that they are worth lots, overriding the property of being worthless (which is the one they would otherwise have inherited from the object frame). All artefacts are light objects:

```
artefact::
    ako : woodobject
    ako : lightobject
    shape : pole
    emanates : magic
```

Wand is ako artefact and ako lightobject. It is on the table:

```
wand::
    ako : artefact
    on : table
```

Paper objects are a kind of object, and are all a kind of light object, too. They're made of paper and all of them are oblong in shape:

```
paperobject::
    ako : object
    ako : lightobject
    made-of : paper
    shape : oblong
```

A book is a paper object, which is worth something:

```
book::
    ako : paperobject
    worth : something
```

Tome is a kind of book. It is on the shelf, and its title is, *Tome of Tricks*. It contains the bookmark:

```
tome::
    ako : book
    on : shelf
    title : 'Tome of Tricks'
    contains : bookmark
```

The bookmark is ako paperobject, and it's inside the tome:

```
bookmark::
    ako : paperobject
    inside : tome
```

Assuming definitions for liquid and potion, potion3 is a potion which is inside bottle3. It is large and green, and maybe it emanates magic:

```
potion3::
    ako : potion
    ako : largeobject
    inside : bottle3
    colour : green
    emanates : magic
```

I could, of course, go on almost indefinitely like this (and so, hopefully, could you!). What we have here is a logical description – a taxonomy – of the wizard's room. Adding new concepts is very straightforward: for example, to think about transparent objects you would just create a new class which is ako object, and which has bottles and liquids as subclasses. A new object, such as a crown, is easily introduced; it's a simple matter to slot it in under metalobject, and to override the value slot with priceless. To extend the range of how much objects can be worth is also easy – most of it is inherited anyway, you only need to change a couple of places! How about removing the bookmark from the tome and putting it on the table? Just get rid of the bookmark's inside property, take it out of the contains slot of the object it was inside (the tome), give it an on slot with value table, and add it to the under slot of table. There it is, moved, with very little difficulty.

Well that just about wraps up this part of the book on knowledge representation. In it, I have introduced you to several notions culled from Artificial Intelligence, and I have tried to stress the benefit which can be gained by using logics and abstract data types properly. Most adventure programmers probably use Frames anyway. However, they don't *know* that they're using Frames, and consequently they can easily misuse them by contaminating them with horrible, hacky procedures, which defeat the purpose of using Frames in the first place.

The next issue to consider is the representation of actions in this system. Actions are intimately entangled with the way in which commands are given. To understand the nature of commands, you need to know what it is people can say to your system, and this means you'll need something capable of understanding a subset of some natural language. Because of this, the next chapter is devoted to that topic.

6
NATURAL LANGUAGE

6.0 SYNTAX AND SEMANTICS

A *natural language* is a language spoken by normal, everyday human beings, such as English, Greek or Urdu. 'Natural language' (NL) is also the name of a vast subfield within AI, the aim of which is to create programs which can 'understand' – in some sense of the word – a natural language.

There are many aspects to NL, covering a wide range of topics. A few of the more interesting ones include machine translation (turning a piece of French text into a passable piece of English text, for example), story-writing, paraphrasing (extracting the meaning from a sentence and re-presenting it in a more understandable fashion) and speech synthesis (where a piece of hardware is driven to produce whistles and whines which a human is able to recognise as meaningful words). All these are very difficult, and even something as innocuous as a spelling corrector program can cause real headaches: in the sentence `Farmer Giles was sowing` *X*, if you replace the *X* with `seeds`, then it is spelled correctly, whereas if you replace it with `socks` then it isn't! If you said `Farmer Giles was sowing some socks with a needle and thread`, then it's *probably* incorrect, although not always – for example it's perfectly OK when used in this sentence you're now reading!

The particular kind of NL with which we will be concerned is primarily that of *parsing*. The bulk of the effort in NL has been devoted to this subject because it is a fundamental precondition for most other parts of the field, in the same way that operations such as obtaining the mean of a set of numbers permeates through virtually all of statistics.

Parsing is the process by which you take an input and try to discover what the user meant by it. In a full-blown NL system, the input would normally be something like unconstrained English, and the users could say anything they wanted. Unfortunately, despite the outpourings of TV scriptwriters, NL understanding on this scale is still a long, long way off. The best we can manage so far requires severe restrictions on the form of the things which people are allowed to say. It is then not necessary to be able to interpret such loopy phrases as 'the sword the man the wizard zapped used broke' (meaning 'the sword, used by the man who was zapped by the wizard, broke'). We often have to restrict the things that the users might wish to talk about, otherwise we would just have to hope that they were never going to say 'pass me a sugar mouse' to a system designed to answer questions about internal combustion engines.

The idea, then, is to define a subset of the natural language which you want to parse, in terms of the way words may reasonably be slotted together to make sense. So, if you think of a *sentence* as consisting of a *verb*, followed by a *noun*, followed by the word 'with', followed by another *noun*, then the sentence `open door with keys` would be fine, but `with keys open door` would not. The rigid format which determines permissible ways in which words can be arranged to form a sentence in a language is called the *syntax* of that language. In theory, you could probably list every sentence that you want your NL system to recognise, but that's going to be a lengthy process – infinitely long in some cases! The solution, instead, is to use a word's *type* so that, instead of saying that you can 'kick ball' or 'kick balloon' or 'burst ball' or 'burst balloon', you define kick and burst as verbs, balloon and ball as nouns and accept a verb followed by a noun.

Words, therefore, will have to be of the right *type* to fit into the syntax, so somewhere you are going to have to have a list of acceptable words, together with their types. This list of words and types is called a *lexicon* or *dictionary*. The set of rules which – in conjunction with this list – describes the syntax of the language, is called its *grammar*. *Parsing* is the process of finding out the function of words in a sentence, while *syntax* is what provides the limits of what is and is not acceptable as input, and a grammar is a set of rules for describing the syntax.

Even taking things at this level of simplicity can cause problems. The entries in the lexicon may also carry an implicit *human* meaning to which the parser has no access. MUD, for example, has an 'American trap' in it, which goes like this:

```
In a misty graveyard there is a tomb,
and a voice speaking inside your head
says a prize will open it
```

Now, since the voice is inside your head, whether it says `prize` or `prise` is non-determined, they both sound the same when *spoken*. So it can be spelled `prize` but mean `prise`. If you type `prise tomb`, the tomb will open.

The trick is that for many speakers of American English, 'prise' is not a word, they use 'pry' instead and thus are never likely to solve the problem. The standard way out of situations where different words have the same meaning is to define them as *synonyms* so that 'pry' and 'prise' will have identical entries in the lexicon. If this were done in the above example, the command `pry tomb` would work although the players would still not be able to figure it out. Obviously, then, the lexicon entries are not enough to *fully* define a word. Part of the meaning of a word lies in its pronounciation and is a property of the *symbol* 'prise' or 'pry', rather than of the *concept* to which they both refer. This kind of information *can* be included in the lexicon, but then there would be no synonyms, instead there would be long lists of word 'meanings' with plenty of sections identical except for the way the symbol sounds.

So, we can have problems at the word level, before even beginning to consider the syntactic structure of a whole sentence! NL understanding is clearly fraught with problems from start to finish.

Syntax defines only the surface structure of a sentence, it says nothing about its meaning. The two sentences `open door with keys` and `flatten water with knife` may both be syntactically correct and, provided the words are all in the lexicon, the program will be able to verify that they *are* both valid sentences in the language. It will probably build up an internal structure which represents the two sentences, maybe a list or an 'ako-tree' (where open is ako verb, door is ako noun, a verb followed by a noun is ako verb phrase, and so on). The parsing process isn't finished yet, however, because we still don't know what the user *intended* by the input. The first sentence, taken as a command, means that the user wants to open a door with some keys, so it might be quite reasonable for the interpreter to try to open some door in its internal representation of the world (the *world model*). The second sentence means, well, it means that you have a very strange view of things!

The 'meaning' of a sentence is called its *semantics*. Semantics, as a concept, is quite hard to grasp, but in essence the semantics of a sentence, command, paragraph or whatever are determined by what you want to be able to *do* with the structure you obtained from the first stage of the parse. In the first sentence shown above, the structure built up from the grammar might be nothing more than the result of assigning values to three variables leaving `action` = open, `object` = door and `instrument` = keys. In this case the semantics might be to look this triple up in a table and execute the code found as a result to complete the parse.

I'll be devoting more space to the subject of of parsing later on, however; a more pressing question which needs to be discussed before going any further concerns the reasons *why* we want to be able to parse natural language in adventure games at all.

6.1 WHERE NATURAL LANGUAGE FITS IN

There are essentially two reasons why NL is a requirement for any self-respecting adventure game. The first is the obvious one that it is easier for humans to give commands to the game if they are able to use more or less everyday language. If that everyday language is too complicated (which of course plain English is), then a reasonable subset should be allowed which *is* capable of being parsed. Surprisingly, there are arguments both for *and* against making the language as free as possible. Most people would be very pleased if they could say what they liked to a game and still be understood – but that's based on their experiences with single-user adventures. In these versions it is probably better to err on the side of free-format input and, if players want to enter commands like `after five seconds, quickly pick up the crystal sphere from behind the bag which contains the furry glove and the spider, and dunk it in the shimmering pool three times`, well then let them – it's their keyboard they are pounding into the ground. In a MUD, though, such verbosity is not encouraged as the player would probably be attacked by a passer-by before the eighth word without ever finishing the sentence! In general, if players understand the basic format of the commands then this offers an additional clue as to how they should phrase the instruction for the action they want to perform. If you know that the parser only takes a verb, a noun, 'with' and an object, then you know that `when the clock strikes twelve open the door with the large key` will not work and that there must be an easier and more effective way to do it.

- If a language makes it hard to say something, then it's a good idea not to try to say it at all.

Another use of NL lies in communication with *mobiles*. A mobile is a computer-controlled object which wanders around the internal world with its own goals and purposes, doing as it pleases. Most adventures have some notion of a mobile, they are often called *Non Player Characters* (NPCs) – a term which I dislike, for reasons which I will discuss shortly.

Theoretically, an ideal mobile could do anything which could be done by a player. Thus, if a player can open a door with some keys, then so can a mobile, and the same would go for picking up treasure, taking it to a repository and scoring points for it. If players want to kill players – or mobiles – then mobiles might reasonably request the same privilege. However, mobiles would need to be pretty sophisticated to do this kind of thing, indeed, making simple plans to carry out what we would consider to be trivial tasks is a whole subfield of AI in its own right (discussed later under 'planning').

One human activity which provides a major stumbling block for mobiles is the business of talking to one another. If you were in an adventure game and you came across someone called Trudy, and speaking to her elicited no reply, then you could guess that Trudy was nothing more than a computer-generated puppet, only there to make the game a bit more interesting by carrying on with a reasonably free hand as though she were another player. The program might dress things up a bit by making speechlessness a part of the context (perhaps the game is set in a POW camp where Trudy is a non English-speaking guard, or it is an interplanetary adventure where Trudy is a bizarre alien unable even to communicate) but this is still obvious to the players. If you really want talking mobiles, then they need some kind of NL interface to make sense of your commands and to generate half-decent responses.

There are two ways for a mobile to behave when someone says something that cannot be understood using normal parsing mechanisms. The first one is for the mobile to come clean and admit that it is just a computer-generated Trudy; this would be a wise solution if, for example, the player asks Trudy 'what did you think of West Bromwich Albion's home performance last night?', which requires real-world knowledge to answer.

The second option is to try and conceal the mobile's true identity for as long as possible, thwarting the player's every attempt to discover whether it is a program or a person. This approach is obviously the more interesting of the two, and the harder since it is, essentially, the Turing Test! It is clear that the syntax of the language to which mobiles can respond has to be very open because players, when talking to other players, feel that they are freed of the syntactic shackles which they are forced to observe when giving commands to the game.

A remark to Trudy such as 'Hello Trudy, how's things?' might be a typical opening question, with Trudy replying in context with something like 'Hi there, I just had a bit of bother with a dryad' rather than 'can you rephrase that, I don't follow'. A *robust* program is one which can withstand any phrases which might be offered, no matter how obscure or badly put. For a mobile the rules might be something like: *Try to parse the sentence normally, but if you can't, then ignore most of it, look only for key words and phrases, and bluff it from there.*

This is the *key-word recognition* technique, and it is roughly the method used by the ELIZA program. If a mobile really *is* incapable of giving a reply, then it can just forget it and shuffle off on other business as quickly as possible.

However, if subjecting a mobile to sudden, way-out questioning is all that it takes to uncover it, then getting a mobile to behave in the same way as a genuine player still leaves us with a problem. An original solution is to arrange things so that a mobile taken beyond its limits can send out a distress signal, and have the sentence patched through to a real human being who is also playing within the game – a *gamesmaster* of some sort. This human then attaches to the mobile, providing the poor beleaguered creature with a convincing 'front'. Now, when the mobile is asked 'what is the capital city of Norway?', it contacts the gamesmaster who uses it to channel back the reply 'Eh? Er, Oslo. OK brainbox, what's the capital of Canada?'.

When a gamesmaster (or anyone else with the appropriate magical abilities) attaches to a mobile and 'plays it' for a while, the mobile acts as a temporary 'player' character, rather than as an NPC. This is why I prefer the term mobile to 'non player character': NPC is just a state of existence mobiles can have.

As far as talking to mobiles is concerned, they might as well be NPCs since, if there is a player in control, you can use the normal, existing communication channels for player/player interaction. Player/mobile (and, indeed, mobile/mobile) conversation in natural language is very interesting, but its reliance on very complex parsing algorithms takes it well beyond the scope of this book. If an interpreter knows that it is only going to be given commands and simple questions (as is the case for the MUD interpreter awaiting players' instructions), then it's far easier to predict the kind of thing people want to say. If you're going to take in the whole gamut of questions, comments, guarded statements, metaphorical phrases, irony, proverbs and all the rest, then your task is going to be massive – well up to Nobel Prize standards! Otherwise, put your mobile on hold running an ELIZA-like program, and hope that some human will attach to it before anyone gets wind of what is really going on!

I won't concern myself with player/mobile conversation much in this book, due to the increased difficulty of the topic – NL parsing of commands is hard enough in itself if you've not had any experience in the area before. I mention the possibility simply so that you know it's there, and that there are ways it can be handled if you're prepared to buy an NL textbook on more general parsing strategies than those outlined here.

A couple of final hints on the topic of mobiles trying to pass themselves off as humans: they should not *always* be around, and they should be able to increase their experience and knowledge – in other words they must be able to learn. Learning is another complex aspect of AI which is touched on later in this book. In fact the interaction between NL use and learning has proven highly problematical and is, as yet, far from properly understood.

6.2 TEXT GENERATION

There is one other part which NL can play in improving a MUD, and for which a MUD provides an interesting application domain, and this is in text generation. If you have your objects defined as *Frames*, then instead of the designer of the world giving objects a 'textual' description (for subsequent use by a procedure `describe-object`), it may be possible to generate the object's description 'on the fly' (ie. in real-time) from its Frame. If an object's Frame looks like this:

```
ball1::
        ako : ball
        colour : red
```

then it would be fine to say 'there is a red ball here'. This assumes that the player knows what a ball is, and is aware of the properties which are likely to be inherited from that Frame (its shape is round, and it is ako `lightobject`). The description can be embellished with pseudo-random phrases so that, instead of 'there is a red ball here', we might get 'a red ball lies over to one side' or 'before you,

you espy a red ball'. It's when you want to say things like 'A red ball has rolled here' that things get interesting, because you need to know the additional fact that balls roll.

You have a choice of ways of dealing with this: you can either build more sophisticated text generation systems for general use, or use the old system but for objects requiring really flashy descriptions, provide a 'description' slot in which you can pre-define as much as you like. This *textual attachment* is very powerful, but may need an incredibly resourceful text generator for it to figure out the correct descriptions: when you drop a ball, it seeks the lowest room before it stops moving, and the name of this action (just one of many possible) is called 'rolling'. You could *tell* it, of course, but then you might as well give the whole description. A far better way is not to bother with text generation at all, and if you want to read information off Frames, then have a picture generator instead, which gives you a graphical interpretation of the object in terms of shape, colour, size and so on.

We are now going to look at the processes by which a command from a user of a MUD system is parsed. The particular approach used here will make use of some of the most powerful techniques of AI and is not, therefore, as simple as this general introduction implies. In the system described, there are *two* parses of a sentence. The 'meaning' of the first parse is a data structure, normally a *tree* which describes the way in which the grammar (representing the syntax) decreed that the parse should proceed – these trees are called *derivation trees* or *parse trees*. The second parse then takes this tree and uses a different grammar to 'map' it into a set of primitive instructions which the interpreter can then execute, to provide the 'meaning' of the overall command. The first parse is a 'shallow', syntactic parse, the second one is a 'deep', more semantic parse.

First, then, I will show a simple method for writing out syntax rules, which may then be used as a grammar. I shall then describe the basic format of MUD commands and try to evolve a syntax with which most of them will conform. Next, I'll outline a method for parsing sentences and apply it to this syntax (the method will, of course, work on other syntaxes as well), using its grammar in a hierarchical manner to generate parse trees. After that I will look at what goes on behind the deep parse, which takes the parse tree and produces a collection of primitive instructions which are then executed. Finally I shall analyse the process and propose a suitable representation for actions in the world model.

6.3 SYNTAX MADE EASY

To start with, then, how do we go about describing the syntax of a language? The scheme most commonly used is called the *Backus-Naur Form* (BNF) after its inventors. Syntax and grammar are interwoven concepts: the difference is that a grammar is a way of describing a syntax, whereas a syntax is a sieve which either accepts or rejects sentences, but does nothing else. The application of rules of grammar to a sentence can be used to construct derivation trees, which are representations of what rules of the grammar were used to accept the input string of words. Hence, it is a good idea to have the rules of the grammar described in such a way as to make using them to parse as easy as possible. BNF offers such a way.

So what does BNF look like? Or, put another way, what is its syntax? Well, consider a BNF fragment such as:

```
<insult> ::= you <obscenity>.
```

BNF consists of a set of rules, called *productions* (or *rewrite rules*), of which the above is an example. The productions come in two parts separated by ::= – a *pattern* and an *expansion*. Patterns and expansions both consist of strings of symbols which are either *terminal* symbols, written as ordinary lower case letters (such as you); or *non-terminal* symbols written in angle brackets < > such as <insult>. One of the non-terminal symbols is defined as the 'start' symbol and is usually <s> or <sentence>. Using this collection of words and symbols it is possible to write a grammar for a language.

Well, not quite yet, because all I've given you so far is the syntax of BNF. To understand it requires the semantics. The ::= sign means: 'If you see something in the sentence which matches what is on the left-hand side, then replace it with what is on the right-hand side'. It is a bit like an implication rule in the Predicate Calculus. Terminal symbols are just words, real ones, which you expect to find in your (English) input sentence; when you match a BNF rule with the input then terminals will only match against themselves. You can arrange these terminals in any number of ways, but only a few of them will actually be sensible – which few is determined by the syntax.

Non-terminal symbols are usually categories of words, or categories of word categories. So <noun> might be a reasonable non-terminal symbol, as might <noun-phrase> (which we'll use later on); <sentence> certainly is! A *syntactic category* of this kind is dubbed a non-terminal symbol because it is not found in the original input sentence, but is instead a shorthand representation of part of an input sentence. So, if I said:

```
<noun> ::= stoat
<noun> ::= weasel
```

then I could use the non-terminal `<noun>` all over the place instead of having to use stoat or weasel or any of the other hundreds of words I might wish to use as nouns. It's as if any time I said `<noun>` it could be expanded into any of the words on the right-hand side of a production in which `<noun>` is on the left-hand side. So I could 'rewrite' `<noun>` as either `stoat` or `weasel` in this example.

BNF allows things like these to be written more easily. Instead of having to use a separate line for every different word, it is possible to put them all into one like this:

```
<noun> ::= [ stoat | weasel ]
```

which says 'a noun is either a stoat or a weasel'. It is short for the two-line version shown previously but is, however, just syntactic sugar really – the other form is equally valid.

It is not necessary to have terminals on the right and non-terminals on the left, you can also mix them up. Here, for example, is a BNF definition of a *noun phrase* which says that a noun phrase is an adjective phrase followed by a noun (an adjective is a word which describes a noun, such as 'big' or 'yellow'). So, a BNF definition of a *noun phrase*:

```
<noun-phrase> ::= <adject-phrase> <noun>
```

You can have any number of things on the right-hand side or, for that matter, on the left. What shall we have as an `<adject-phrase>`? How about either nothing at all, or an adjective followed by an `<adject-phrase>`:

```
<adject-phrase> ::= [ <adjective>
                      <adject-phrase> | 0 ]
```

The symbol 0 means *empty production*, and says that you can replace the symbols to the left of `::=` with nothing at all if you like (just get rid of them). It is a good idea, generally, to avoid 0s because they are pretty difficult to follow and can cause problems in parsing later on.

The definition of an `<adject-phrase>`, by the way, is *right-recursive*, it includes a reference to itself on the right-hand side of a terminal/non-terminal pair. A *left-recursive* definition would be:

```
<subject-phrase> ::= [ <adject-phrase>
                       <adjective> | 0 ]
```

which says the same thing but in a different way. Rather than reading 'An `<adjective phrase>` is an `<adjective>` followed by another `<adjective phrase>`', it now says 'an `<adjective phrase>` is an `<adjective phrase>` followed by an `<adjective>`'. The right-recursive form is preferred because if you imagine a program trying to use these rules, it would forever be looking at the same non-terminal symbol, <adject-phrase>, and never finishing. At least with the right-recursive form it will 'bottom out' when it comes across something which isn't an adjective.

To make this kind of thing easier, BNF has another piece of syntactic sugar: the symbol * after anything means 'any number of occurrences of this, including none'. So:

```
<adject-phrase> ::= <adjective>*
```

means 'an `<adjective phrase>` is any number of `<adjective>`s'. This, again, is just a shorthand for the right-recursive form. Right-recursion is sometimes called *tail recursion* and it can be replaced by iteration. In a normal programming language, for example, the control structure:

```
while <test> do <command>
```

is the same as:

```
if <test> then
begin
     <command>
     while <test> do <command>
end.
```

The name tail recursion originates from use in the AI language LISP which has proved to be the most popular of all AI languages over the years, especially in the USA.

There is one other piece of BNF to consider before looking more closely at grammars, and that is the ? construct. Suppose I decided that a `<noun phrase>` was a `<determiner>` word (like 'the' or 'a' or 'an'), followed by any number of `<adjectives>`, ('red', 'heavy', 'smelly') followed by a `<noun>` ('stoat', 'book', 'octopus'). We get this:

```
<noun-phrase> ::= <determiner>
                  <adjective>* <noun>
```

I've dropped the `<adjective-phrase>` here and just put the `<adjective>*` in straight by itself. Imagine I now want to change this so that instead of just understanding strings of words of the form 'the red octopus' or 'the smelly heavy book' or 'a stoat', I could just take 'red octopus' or 'smelly heavy book' or 'stoat'. I can't use `<determiner>*` here because that would allow sentences like 'the an the red book', and I want to limit it to one or zero occurrences of `<determiner>`. That's where the ? comes in:

```
<noun-phrase> ::= <determiner>?
                  <adjective>* <noun>
```

means 'a `<noun phrase>` is either 0 or 1 `<determiners>` followed by any number of `<adjectives>`, followed by a `<noun>`'.

BNF, then, provides a way of describing the ways in which sentences can be constructed, without having to list them all explicitly (which would be impossible anyway when they may be of arbitrary length). BNF rules cover more sentences than are ever likely to be typed in, and because they're syntactic there's no meaning behind any of the words as far as the BNF is concerned. They are used solely for describing what is or isn't a satisfactory input. Even if it proves syntactically correct, a sentence may still be rejected later on by the semantic part of the parse. 'Crush neon with wren' may be syntactically correct, but has little meaning in the real world! Still, it *could* be acceptable in an adventure!

6.4 PARSING WITH BNF

Armed with this BNF way of representing grammars, we can do quite a lot. How do we use them to parse a sentence, though? Well there are two ways to do it: either forward-running ('top-down') or backward-running ('bottom-up'). Top-down means you start with the topmost non-terminal – the start symbol (which as I said earlier is going to be either `<sentence>` or `<s>`, by convention) – and you look for all the possible ways you could expand it. This means you look up `<sentence>` or `<s>` on the left-hand side of the `::=` and replace it with whatever is on the right-hand side. This will give you a new set of symbols, and you expand those all possible ways – and so on until you have a set of terminal symbols which match the input.

Bottom-up parsing is where you take the input sentence and try to match it against the right-hand side of the `::=` and, when a match is found, replace it with the left-hand side, continuing until you have only one symbol left, the start symbol (except of course it is now at the *end* of what you do here!).

As an example of these two, here's a grammar for a simple language:

```
<noun>         ::= [ sword | axe | knife
                   | mace ]
<adjective>    ::= [ shiny | heavy
                   | valuable  | sharp]
<determiner>   ::= [ the | a | any ]
<verb>         ::= [ drop | describe
                   | get | break ]
```

```
<adverb>       ::= [ quickly | slowly
                   | cautiously ]
<noun-phrase> ::= <determiner>?
                   <adjective>*<noun>
<verb-phrase> ::= [ <verb> <adverb>
                   | <adverb> <verb> ]
<sentence>     ::= <verb-phrase> <noun>?
```

The first four lines define some common parts of speech, the rest describe how to stick them together. The last line indicates that a `<sentence>` consists of a `<verb phrase>` optionally followed by a `<noun phrase>`. If we obtained the input string 'quickly drop the valuable shiny knife' then we could use the grammar in a top-down fashion through the following steps:

replace: `<sentence>` *with* `<verb-phrase>`
`<nounphrase>`
to get: `<verb-phrase> <noun-phrase>`

replace: `<verb-phrase>` *with* `<adverb> <verb>`
to get: `<adverb> <verb> <noun-phrase>`

replace: `<adverb>` *with* `quickly`
to get: `quickly <verb> <noun-phrase>`

replace: `<verb>` *with* `drop`
to get: `quickly drop <noun-phrase>`

replace: `<noun-phrase>` *with* `<determiner>`
`<adjective> <noun>`
to get: `quickly drop <determiner> <adjective> <noun>`

replace: `<determiner>` *with* `the`
to get: `quickly drop the <adjective> <noun>`

replace: `<adjective>` *with* `valuable <adjective>`
to get: `quickly drop the valuable <adjective> <noun>`

replace: `<adjective>` *with* `shiny`
to get: `quickly drop the valuable shiny <noun>n`

replace: `<noun>` *with* `knife`
to get: `quickly drop the valuable shiny knife`

This matches the input sentence. Of course, it's a perfect parse – in reality we'd have tried to generate things like:

replace: `<noun>` *with* `sword`
to get: `quickly drop the valuable shiny sword`

only to find it didn't match at the terminal level, so we'd have to backtrack and try an alternative expansion of `<noun>`. However, the above should be enough to give you the overall gist of what happens.

Parsing in a bottom-up fashion, you work the other way round, starting from the input and trying to get to `<sentence>`. For this kind of parsing, `::=` means 'if you can match the right-hand side against the input, you can replace the matching symbols by the left-hand side'.

replace: `knife` *with* `<noun>`
to get: `quickly drop the valuable shiny <noun>`

replace: `shiny` *with* `<adjective>`
to get: `quickly drop the valuable <adjective> <noun>`

replace: `valuable <adjective>` *with* `<adjective>`
to get: `quickly drop the <adjective> <noun>`

replace: `the` *with* `<determinator>`
to get: `quickly drop <determinator> <adjective> <noun>`

replace: `<determinator> <adjective> <noun>` *with* `<noun-phrase>`
to get: `quickly drop <noun-phrase>`

replace: `drop` *with* `<verb>`
to get: `quickly <verb> <noun-phrase>`

replace: `quickly` *with* `<adverb>`
to get: `<adverb> <verb> <noun-phrase>`

replace: `<adverb> <verb>` *with* `<verb-phrase>`
to get: `<verb-phrase> <noun-phrase>`

replace: `<verb-phrase> <noun-phrase>` *with* `<sentence>`
to get: `<sentence>`

which ends in the start symbol, `<sentence>`, and that terminates our parse!

These simple examples show how the rules in BNF can be applied. Actually, what is described here is a type of *production system*, a production system being a powerful AI tool consisting of sets of *if/then* rules which are usually used as a control strategy (what to do next), but which apply equally well in many other cases, as in this one. I won't go into details in this book, but I thought you'd like to know about them.

The parse was easy here for two reasons: firstly, none of the terminal symbols had more than one meaning. If I had introduced a word 'wind' and said it was a noun ('the wind blew') and a verb ('please wind up the clock') then the bottom-up parse would have been flummoxed, and may have got quite far before finding out that it had made a mistake and would have had to backtrack to the point where it erred and then take the other alternative. Even human beings can make a wrong initial choice – most people would do a double-take when faced with 'the old shed tears alone' or 'the firm's bank reserves interest benefits for long-standing customers'. If several choices between alternative rewrites are available and the first is always taken, then it is a *depth-first* search. A *breadth-first* search is where all the alternatives are taken and expanded through one step, then these expansions are too. Depth-first is faster for short sentences and doesn't use as much memory. However, it can make a mess of productions like this:

```
<sentence> ::=
[<sentence> and <sentence> | <verb-phrase>
                    <noun-phrase>]
```

There it would keep trying to expand a sentence only to get the same non-terminal back first every time – which it also tries to expand, coming up with yet another identical expansion, *ad infinitum*! At least breadth-first gets the two sides of the | expanded at the same time, in parallel, so it will win out even on left-recursive definitions like the above.

6.5 TYPES OF GRAMMAR

One reason why the parse in the previous section is so easy is because the grammar was easy. There are several different classes of grammar, ranging from the easy-to-implement but not over-expressive to the richly expressive grammars which are nightmarish to implement.

Everyone working in the field recognises the following classification of grammars, due to the linguist Chomsky who first worked in this area. The classes are numbered type 0 through to type 3, type 3 being the easy one and type 0 being the hard one, with types 1 and 2 lying somewhere in between. Languages described by grammars of these four types are themselves said to be of that numbered type: a language with a type 3 grammar is a type 3 language.

Type 3 grammars, or 'regular grammars', contain productions only of the form:

```
P ::= z Q
```

or

```
P ::= z
```

where `P` and `Q` are any single non-terminals and `z` is any terminal. The grammar we looked at earlier was not of that form, because we had two or three things on the right-hand side of the `::=` – although if you wanted to, you could probably write it as a type 3 grammar (the syntax would be the same, accepting the same set of input sentences, but the grammar would be different). Regular grammars may be rather short and inexpressive, but they are very simple to implement.

Type 2 grammars are known as *context free grammars*, a term which means that you can't restrict replacing non-terminals by their expansions only to a few select situations, you either have to allow it for every case, or not at all. This kind of grammar contains productions which have only a single non-terminal on their left-hand side, but anything at all on the right. Obviously, then, type 3 grammars are also type 2. A cursory glance at the grammar I produced earlier shows that it is type 2. Context free grammars are also very easy to parse, and most conventional programming languages are described by grammars of this sort.

Type 1 grammars are *context sensitive grammars*, so called because they can have a context on the left-hand side. This means that you can put a non-terminal on the left-hand side of the `::=`, embedded between two (possibly empty) strings of other terminals and non-terminals. On the right-hand side, you have the same collection of these other symbols, but with the single one replaced by an expansion. So:

```
open <determiner> <noun> please ::= open
that <noun> please
```

would be acceptable. Type 2 grammars are type 1 grammars with an 'empty' context, they have no strings either side of the left-hand non-terminal. Writing a parser for a context-sensitive grammar is very difficult, as is getting a grammar for them in the first place. Most natural languages are at least type 1.

Type 0 grammars don't have any extra special name, and they have no restrictions on what kind of rewrite rules you use for them. If you want to be able to replace all occurrences of `<name> and <name>` by `mr. and mrs.` then you can do, using

```
<name> and <name> ::= mr. and mrs.
```

It's pretty obvious that all grammars are of type 0, whatever else they may be. Type 0 grammars are notoriously difficult to parse, and there is no known mechanistic way of parsing them other than trying all productions in turn, in a breadth-first fashion. Type 0 grammars can be used to describe any transformations which are, in theory, computationally possible (given enough time to do them).

To examine the relative powers of these grammars or – more to the point for three of them – their lack of power, let's just take a quick look at what kind of thing they can be used to generate by a top-down expansion. Say we wanted to create sequences of identical words, which for convenience we will represent as the single letters `x` and `y`. The kinds of sequences we can build up depend on the power of the grammar we use. A regular grammar can manage a series of `x`'s followed by `y`'s, as in `x x x x y y y y y`, but it can't produce a series which guarantees the same number of `x`'s and `y`'s. A context free grammar can make the two strings the same length, as in `x x x x y y y y`, but it can only do it for two different words. A context sensitive grammar can get you constant-length sequences for any number of different letters, as in `x x x x y y y y z z z z`. Type 0 grammars, though, can produce absolutely anything, for example counting using alternate `x`'s and `y`'s `x y y x x x y y y y x x x x x`.

This book virtually ignores type 0 grammars – they're just too hard. Mainstream linguists, some of whom are struggling to produce a full grammar for English (and not managing it very well) agree, too! Type 3 grammars are too easy, and you can't say much in them anyway.

Type 1 and 2 grammars, however, are more interesting. They're collectively known as *phrase-structure* grammars, because you can build a structure from the production rule phrases which you used in parsing. If you think back to the sequence of parsing operations used for the sentence 'quickly drop the valuable shiny knife', you can draw an hierarchical structure where each of the words is below the rule which was used to derive it, each of these is below the rule by which it was generated itself, and so on up to the root which is `<sentence>`. The resulting structure, shown in Figure 6.1, is the *derivation tree* mentioned earlier. The vertical lines act like a `::=`, so that if there was more than one symbol on its right, then they would all be children of the non-terminal which appeared on its left, connected to it by vertical lines in order of appearance. It's pretty self-evident when you look at it. Note that we end up with the same tree no matter whether we decide to do a top-down parse or a bottom-up one. You can, from the diagram, see how terminal symbols and non-terminal symbols get their respective names.

Derivation trees are very useful, and we'll be aiming to get one which we can use in a MUD. Our objective, once we've outlined this structure, is to read off a few things – such as the verb, what are the relevant adverbs and what are the objects to which the verb should be applied – and then to proceed onto a deep parse which ties these into the semantics of the language, ie. which actually does something. This structure-to-rules relationship is very important and needs to be remembered!

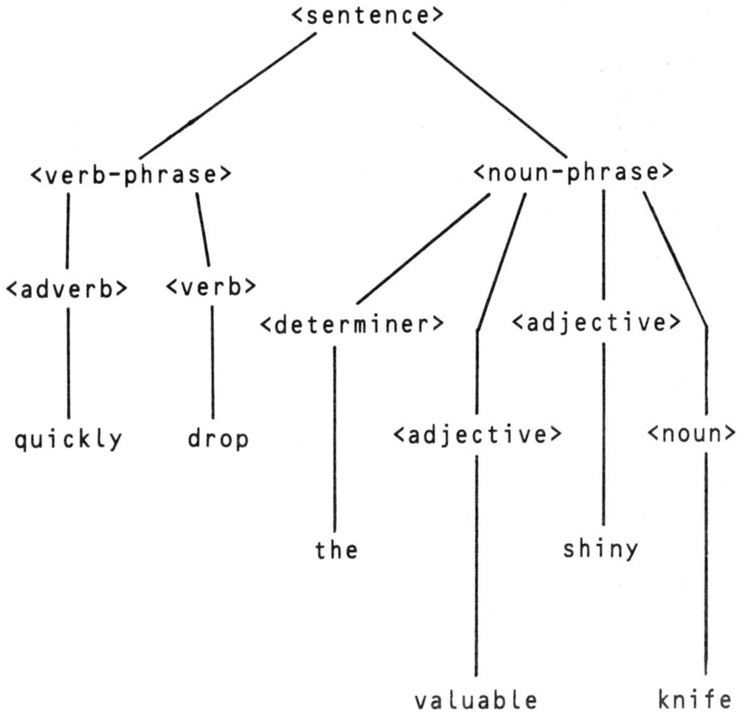

Figure 6.1 Derivation tree

6.6 PARSING ADVENTURE GAME COMMANDS

Adventures are quite a fortunate class of programs as far as writing natural language interfaces is concerned, in that most of the things which you want to convey to them are of the same sort: the *imperative sentence* (or *command*). What you might want to say to mobiles is another matter, but to the main interpreter the input is always going to be a command of some kind. (Unless there's some fancy switching mechanism which allows things like 'treat everything I say as if it had a *shout* command in front of it', which might be useful for conversations with other players, say.)

Even the questions you will want to ask can be couched in terms of commands, so 'where ox?' has a verb part of 'where' and an object part of 'ox', in the same manner as 'stroke ox' has a verb of 'stroke' and an object of 'ox', even though 'where' is really an adverb modifying the verb 'is' (not present in this example). Rather than use the word 'verb' here, though, I'll call it an *action*, to get away from the linguistic labels and stop any pedantic readers from baulking every time they see some use of a grammatical term which they don't like! In particular, an action may end up being constructed out of the verb together with a number of adverbs ('go quickly' is the same as 'run', for example). Later on I'll be introducing a few other names for use in our system, which go with action.

The process of *lexical analysis* splits sentences into words by ignoring spaces, tabs and the like; it converts all letters to the same case (UPPER or lower), and I shall not detail it here. It's pretty easy to write a function which reads in and identifies a word, looks it up in the dictionary, and returns a pointer to a dictionary entry giving a list of possible meanings of that word. Every system needs such a module and a great deal of the processing time spent in understanding natural language is taken up merely by normalising the input sentences into distinct words instead of an otherwise meaningless stream of ASCII characters!

So what kind of sentence do we want to be able to input? An elaborate example of what we'd hope to be able to understand in an all-singing, all-dancing system might be something like:

```
after 3 seconds, quickly open all three
orange boxes by using the largest of the
steel spikes in the rucksack, then knock
on all the doors except the biggest one
twice
```

Well, that just about covers it! If you can parse sentences like that, then you can parse just about anything that is reasonably likely to come up in a MUD!

Looking at this command, we see that it is actually two commands separated by the conjunction, 'then'. We can ignore most of the punctuation or include it in the form of words (comma and dot) if we wanted to be really pedantic. Next we can break the commands up into 5 fragments: *delay, action, objects, instruments* and *repetitions*. So for the first command we would get (3 seconds), (quickly open), (all 3 orange boxes), (largest of steel spikes in rucksack), (once). For the second we would get (0 seconds), (knock), (all doors except biggest one), (), (twice).

What we have after breaking the sentence up in this way is the *result* of a shallow parse. The way it is shown here is a bit informal, but it is still what we're aiming for. The idea is that the users might give the same command several ways, and we have to make sure that whichever way they choose, it boils down to the same set of sentential elements. So 'silently pick up the small knife', 'pick the small knife up silently', 'pick up silently the knife which is small' and 'silently pick the knife which is small up' would all produce the same deep structure of (0 seconds), (pick up silently), (small knife), (), (once).

The purpose of the following sections is to come up with something which will get us as far as this. To do it, we'll have to devise some kind of syntax for the commands we hope to be able to understand – BNF will help us considerably here. Then in the next chapter we can try to use our BNF description as a grammar and find a parsing algorithm.

6.7 PROBLEMS IN PARSING

First of all, though, I'd better point something out. Natural language is a very big area of AI, and there are many different ways to parse sentences. Different grammars abound, and everyone has their favourite. There are too many to describe in a book of this nature, so I have opted for a particular halfway-house kind of parse which uses two of the most popular parsing techniques, one for the shallow parse and one for the deep parse. Actually, there are sound theoretical reasons for doing it this way, especially if you want to be able to understand several different languages without making it hard for yourself (you just rewrite the shallow part).

However, another, more practical, reason is that if you were producing this kind of thing for a MUD, the shallow parse (which got you to the five parts of the sentence) would be basically transportable; so if you designed several radically different adventures, the same parsing mechanism would be able to get you to the five components. The only knowledge of the vocabulary that you would need would be the words allowed and what parts of speech they are (verb, adjective, noun, adverb, and so on – or even several at once). This would mean that a lot of the parsing work, the shallow parse, could be done remotely on the user's micro. Only the results of the shallow parse need be passed over the connecting communication lines to the deep parser running on the MUD host machine. This cuts down the amount of information which has to be sent, and reduces the workload on the central computer because it is just given the five stripped-down components, and needn't bother with the mundane task of finding out what the individual words in the original sentence meant.

There are disadvantages to this method, however. In particular, if all you know about a word is its type, then there are some sentences which you'll mis-parse. The worst case is where you have an ambiguity which you can't sort out until you get to the deep parse stage. If I said 'get the ball on the table' then that (normally) means the action is get, and the object is the ball on the table. If I say 'drop the ball on the table' it is usually the same as ' drop on the table the ball which I am holding'. So our five components for the get case would be (0 seconds), (get), (ball on table), (), (once). For the drop case they'd be (0 seconds), (drop), (ball), (table), (once). But get and drop are both verbs, and if verbs are treated generically then we're going to make an error in at least one case ('where do you want the ball on the table to be dropped, please?'). So how do we know which one to do? We can't tell until we know more about get and drop, and when doing a shallow parse all we know about them is their type, namely verb. To get round it we can produce *two* types of verb: ones which try to have an object and an instrument, and ones which just have the object (and use the second object mentioned, the table, as the means by which to select from the many possible balls there may be). The solution I shall employ here, to keep it simple, is just to ignore the problem and pick the one which is easiest to do in the parser. After all, the sentence really *is* ambiguous and if the user meant something different, well, they should have been more careful about how they phrased it!

As it turns out, that's not too much of a hindrance. People tend not to use sophisticated commands in adventures anyway, and some of the five slots in the structure will frequently have to be filled in with defaults (the main effect will be that we want to do whatever it is we're told to do after 0 seconds, and it will do it once only).

There are many examples of this kind of ambiguity in real life, for example newspaper headlines declaring 'Police shoot man with knife' or 'Monty flies back to front' (an attempt to describe General Montgomery's return to the fighting lines in World War Two). You can see plenty of these in collections of awful errors, both from printing and from the TV ('I watched the Argentinians eating food through my binoculars'). Although there exist ways to get round this sort of problem, which is called *pp-attachment* (*pp* stands for *prepositional phrase*), they are inevitably cumbersome and certainly not very clear to the non-expert, so I shall ignore them as much as possible here and trust the user to be clear at all times!

Trusting the user, by the way, isn't as unwise a thing to do as it sounds. You can get away with murder while parsing if you can be fairly sure that the sentences you'll be given are going to be correct reasonably often, and ambiguous hardly ever. That's the case with adventures. The parser used in the original MUD dismissed completely words like 'the' and 'a' as *noise words*, and you were wasting your time if you typed them. It assumed the format would be:

```
<action> <object> <anything at all> <instrument>
```

so that 'open door with keys' might as well be 'open door screwdriver keys' or 'open door hjhkhjhk keys' for all that the system cared. If it was given only three words, it ignored the middle one ('open kitchen door' is the same as 'open door'), and that was just about as sophisticated as it got! It could handle `with <instrument> <action> <object>`, but precious little else. However, because users generally wanted to say only a small number of things, and the command format is always the same, MUD's parser coped remarkably well.

Furthermore, a lot of people were actually quite impressed by MUD's parser, even though it was only for a type 3 subset of English, not even scraping type 2 power! It has been reported as better than that of the mighty ZORK, despite the fact that it was less than fifty lines long. This power was actually quite illusory, and was due to the intelligence of the players rather than that of the program. It would react properly to sentences like `kill the bunny rabbit then drop it in the bag`, which looks quite good; the pronoun 'it' was only a pointer to the last noun mentioned, but this still gave the appearance of a sophisticated program concept!

Abbreviations added to the effect. The above rabbit-slaughtering session could be shortened to `k rabbit. dr it i bag`. A lot depends on the players, though, and common sentences which MUD couldn't handle include 'pick the coin up' (instead of 'pick up the coin', which was OK); 'close the door quietly' (it could manage 'close quietly the door'); 'drop all except the axe' (you had to 'keep axe then drop all') and 'open the kitchen door with the shiny key' (only one adjective, ie. kitchen or shiny, would be accepted). Still, MUD succeeded quite well despite this comparatively rudimentary NL interface, and allowed reasonably free input sentences.

There are genuine problems if you start making things *too* free. The more sentence structures you are prepared to accept, the easier it becomes for phrases to be taken ambiguously, even when they're not really ambiguous at all. If we decided that it was unlikely that someone is going to get a mis-match between plural and singular forms (ie. not likely to say anything like 'drop all the vegetables which is green' rather than 'drop all the vegetables which are green') then that's probably fair enough. It means we can treat words like 'is' and 'are' as if they were the same, and cut down the number of rules in our syntax (and hence reduce the time it takes to parse input). We must be wary, however, of 'kill the sheep which is largest' and 'kill the sheep which are largest'. If we had four sheep, then in the first case we want to kill just the largest one, and in the second we want to kill several of the largest – certainly more than one. So if you relax the constraints you're prepared to accept on the input, then you are also opening the door to ambiguity and possible misinterpretation. The problem in this example arises because the word 'sheep' is both a singular and plural noun.

It's actually quite a lot of bother to keep tabs on this sort of thing, and it is probably not worth the effort for the case of mistaking singular and plural forms of nouns. If we default to assuming the singular, then they can always make sure it does more than one by saying 'kill the largest sheep, three times' (although even this assumes that you don't want to kill the *same* sheep three times!). Sometimes we'll still trip up for when the same word is the singular for one object and the plural for another: 'fetch me some buttons!' and 'fetch me a buttons' mean different things if you're working on the pantomime Cinderella! We'd have been able to get it if 'buttons' had been 'Buttons', but our lexical analyser transforms all letters to lower case (or upper case).

So we'll assume, then, that we needn't check on agreement between the plurality of objects and phrases which reference them. This immediately reduces the amount of work to be done quite considerably.

We now have to decide on the different ways in which we could say our five sentential components, write fragments of BNF to encapsulate them, and then look at how to put these pieces together. Rather than actually giving definitions for words and their parts of speech, I'll stay at the linguistic level. Hence, 'noun' will be a terminal symbol rather than a non-terminal, so I don't need to give a full list of nouns like:

```
<noun> ::= [ banana | shuttlecock | doll
           | maypole | ... ]
```

We'll assume that this has been done already, so `noun`, `verb`, `adverb` and the rest would all be terminals in this grammar. We'll have a few examples, though, for the more obscure word catagories (and for ones I've invented myself!).

6.8 FINDING WORDS FOR SLOTS

Let's start with the *delay* slot, then. What are the different ways in which we could phrase something which indicates *when* we want our action to be performed? The easiest thing to do is think up a few examples, so we'll invent some which delay the execution of the action 'laugh' (which might perhaps send a message to everyone in the room informing them that you've laughed). Here are a few example sentences:

```
Wait for a few seconds and then laugh
Pause a moment and then laugh
After 5 minutes do a laugh
Give a laugh every ten seconds
Laugh after a few moments
Wait several seconds then laugh
```

They look pretty much like the kind of thing we might expect to be typed in as part of an input line. We might also see variations like 'When 5 minutes are up laugh', but that's much less likely than the more normal constructions listed above. They're easy enough to include, though, if that's what we want.

Let's say laugh is an example of an `<action>`, although `<action>` will probably be much more complex than just a verb when we get around to defining it. If we break up the first two sentences, and the last one, we'll see they're of the form:

```
<actiong> ::=
[ wait | pause ] for? <length of time>
and? then <action>
```

I've used the word `<actiong>` to stand for *action group*, ie. a group of phrases about an action. We can get around the `and? then` bit by making them both of the type `conj`, for conjunction – although this will be a terminal in our final grammar, I'll put it in `computer type` to remind us that it's actually what the lexical analyser *found* for a word in a lexicon, rather than be the word itself. The sequence `conj conj? <action>` becomes a `conjg`, for *conjunctive group* because, thinking ahead, we'll probably need something like that to handle conjunctions at the sentence level (as in 'laugh then cry').

The words 'wait' and 'pause' are both adverbs, we call them wadv for *wait adverbs*, otherwise we'd let in the whole gamut of other adverbs, like 'quickly' or 'accidentally', which we don't want. Since we don't want real words in our grammar, we'd better give a category name for the word 'for' which occurs in our definition of <actiong>; we'll call it a wprep, meaning *wait preposition*.

We'll have to decide what this <length of time> non-terminal expands to, too (let's shorten its name to the more manageable <length> first, though!). Looking at our sentences, we seem to have two sorts: accurate ones, where we give a precise number of seconds or whatever; and vague ones, where we just say 'a few', or 'several' seconds. It looks like we have the same sort of thing at the end in both cases, a unit, which will be something like 'seconds', 'minutes', 'moment' or 'while'.

The <timea> (*accurate time*) is easy, it is simply a number followed by a unit. We'll also have a number type which includes things like 'ten', '10', and 'single'. We'll ignore plural forms, so number and unit don't have to match – 'one seconds' will be perfectly acceptable in this system. We can also miss out the number if we like and default it to the value 1 (as in 'laugh every second'). The <timev> (*vague time*) consists of an indirect object indobj, such as 'a' or 'an' or 'some', optionally followed by a wprep (like 'few') and a unit.

So on the basis of the first two and the last one of our example sentences, we end up with the following BNF definition:

```
<actiong> ::= wadv wprep? <length> <conjg>?
<length> ::= <timea> | <timev>
<timea> ::= number? unit
<timev> ::= indobj wadj? unit
<conjg> ::= conj conj? <action>
```

Our lexicon would include entries to say that 'for' was a wprep, 'pause' and 'wait' were wadv's, and 'few' was a wadj, and so on.

We haven't given a BNF definition of an <action> yet, we're still considering the delay component of the sentence. However, what we have is still not the whole story because there were three other representative examples we wanted to be able to parse. We've already done some work which will enable us to break them down a bit, and if we rewrite the examples so as to include the fragments already written, we end up with:

After <length> do a <action>
Give a <action> every <length>
and
<action> after <length>.

It's obvious from this that the *do a* and *give a* parts are common, so we'll invent up a non-terminal which we'll call `<wqual>` for *wait qualifier*. A `<wqual>` is `wverb` (a wait verb, like 'do' or 'perform' or 'execute') followed by an `indobj`. We won't bundle it up with `<action>` though, even if they *do* always occur together, because the `<wqual>` is optional. We could, if we wanted, create a `<waction>` it make it all neater.

The only other words we have are `after` and `every`, which are both adverbs. `every` isn't exactly a delay, it's a repetition, which means you redo it after the time is up. 'After' means you do it once only, *after* the time has passed. `every` and `each` are examples of a `radv`, then, and `after` is an `oadv`. Let's stick these together and call them a `<when>`. A `<when>`, followed by either a `<timea>` or a `<timev>` (ie. a `<length>`) becomes a *when group*, `<wheng>`.

Our only remaining problem is to arrange it so that it doesn't matter whether the `<when>` appears first or second. This is easy enough, we use two more productions called `<whenfirst>` and `<when-second>` which have them in their appropriate places.

We are now in a position to write out the whole set of productions for the delay section of the syntax, which I shall do shortly. Remember, though, that since `<actiong>` includes the `<action>` which we shall be performing (and which I have yet to elaborate), and because the delay is actually optional, then one of the possible expansions of `<actiong>` should be `<action>` – without any delay type words mentioned at all. This is included in the first line of the following BNF:

```
<actiong> ::=
wadv wprep? <length> <conjg>? | <whenfirst>
| <whensecond> | <action>
<length> ::= <timea> | <timev>
<timea>  ::= number? unit
<timev>  ::= indobj wadj? unit
<conjg>  ::= conj conj? <action>
<whenfirst> ::= <wheng> conj? <wqual>?
                <action>
<wheng>  ::= <when> <length>
<when> ::= oadv | radv
<wqual> ::= wverb indobj?
<whensecond> ::= <wqual>? <action> <wheng>
```

The above, then, characterises the syntax of the delay slot we're after. The only missing part is the `<action>`, which we still need to define.

6.9 BUILDING THE SYNTAX

The last section went into great detail about delay, and it took quite a time to describe (although I skipped a few bits at the very end). We can apply the same sort of method to the rest of the sentences we want to understand. The next slot I'll do is the last one, for the number of repetitions which should be performed. This is almost unbelievably trivial because all you can really say is something like 'once', 'twice', 'three times', 'four times' and so on. So the adverbs 'once' and 'twice' (and maybe we'd want a 'thrice') take the name tadverbs (*time adverbs*). The other possible phrasing is number followed by <tnoun> (meaning a *time noun* which will cover the words 'times' and 'time'). So a <repeat> is simply defined as:

```
<repeat> ::= tadverb | number tnoun
```

We still need slots for objects and instruments. Objects and instruments will both be parsable using the same syntax, because it doesn't matter where in the sentence you might want to say something like 'the wicked witch' (either as an object or an instrument) it will still be described using the same syntax rules. Let's get a few of the higher-level things out of the way first, like being able to string sentences together. We'll call a sentence a *phrase* (ie. a command) followed by at least one conjunction, followed by a sentence. We will redefine <conjg> as:

```
<conjg> ::= conj conj? <phrase>
```

so that we can then say that a sentence is a phrase followed by any number of <conjg>s. Our old use of <conjg>, in the earlier definition of an <actiong> doesn't lose anything because of this, so we can state:

```
<sentence> ::= <phrase> <conjg>*
```

And what is a phrase? Well, this is just an <actiong>. We could probably put an optional <repeat> before it, for sentences like 'twice kick the snowman', or we could put it after too 'kick the snowman twice' which reads even better. These are also good places to put ordinary adverbs, as in 'quickly kick the snowman' and 'kick the snowman quickly'. Let's stick a <repeat> and an adverb together and call this a *verb qualifier group*, a <vqg>. We can now put into BNF the fact that a phrase is any number of <vqg>s, followed by an <actiong>, followed by any number of <vqg>s. So let's do that:

```
<phrase> ::= <vqg>* <actiong> <vqg>*
```

Now we *only* have to decide what an <action> looks like, and we've finished!

You're probably quite bored enough now at my one-stepping through how definitions are thought up, so I'll be very sketchy as I whisk us through to the final syntax, to save you further agonies at what should, by now, be a fairly obvious process.

We'll allow three action forms, corresponding to:

```
insert the ball in the bag
insert in the bag the ball
in the bag insert the ball
```

The first is <verb> <object> <how> <instrument>, the second one is <verb> <how> <instrument> <object>, and the third is <how> <instrument> <verb> <object>. There are a few ?s we can put in these, for example 'give the man the camel' doesn't have the <how> that's present in 'give to the man the camel'.We could also add a sprinkling of <vqg>s, to cover 'write quickly the letter with the pen' and 'write the letter quickly with the pen'. Other places are handled higher up at the phrase level, although we could, if we liked, bring them down to this level and not pay too much attention to the subsequent increase in the number of ambiguous sentences this might allow. I'll call these three alternative definitions of an action the <verbobjins>, <verbinsobj> and <insverbobj> forms. There are also the variants where you don't have *any* objects (laugh), where you don't have any instrument (close the door), and where you mix in a <how> for the one-object case (laugh at Jonah). We can make all these fit in with a bit of fiddling, but the hard part comes in defining <how>, <verb>, <object> and <instrument>.

The <how> is a connecting preposition between the <object> and the <instrument>. It could be an ordinary preposition (with, at, in, inside etc.), or the preposition 'by' followed by a participle (as in by using or by employing). You can drop the 'by' if you like and just have the participle. 'By' I'll call a *how preposition*, hprep. So:

```
<how> ::= prep | hprep? ptcple
```

It's easy to put in something to parse a <verb>, because this is a syntactic category in itself, so it's really just verb. <object> and <instrument> both make references to nouns, so we'll have an <objg> (*object group*) non-terminal to use for both of them.

All that is left to do is to define what an <objg> is. First of all, an objg is a group of objects, like 'the sword, axe, dagger and cactus', which we could say was a list of noun groups, <ng>s, connected by optional conjs. The usual linguistic name for an <objg>, by the way, is a *noun phrase*, which I used in a rather more restricted way earlier on. <objg> is, however, more in keeping with the grammar I am designing.

So now we're talking about individual objects. What kind of description are we going to allow for them? Well, we'll allow things of the type `string`, to let people use commands such as 'say "hello you old goat" to William', without our having to parse the bits between quotes, they are just a string. Let's look at some other, more substantial, examples of noun groups, which might be handy in a MUD:

```
all the large, green and heavy apples in the wooden
box

four of the 20 largest of the 76 fierce dalmations
except for the
brown one

the least smelly of the five fishes which are on the
table

the square cake which is not pink

the one which is most edible

all of them but the radiator
```

A nice selection of complicated things there. If you look at them for long enough, you'll see they are really all the same kind of thing, fitting snugly into the following format:

```
<ng> ::= <count>? <adjg>* <identity> <augment>?
```

where `<adjg>*` is a list of adjectives with or without conjunctions between them, and `<identity>` is either a `noun`, a `pronoun` or a `number`. The other two we'll have to describe in more detail.

`<count>` refers to the number of the objects you want to work with, so if there are four cats in the room you might want to work with one, two, three or all four. The simplest case, apart from not mentioning it at all, is where you just say 'a' or 'one' or 'any' – an indefinite object or `indef`. You don't care which cat you get, any will do (they all taste the same!). If you want to be vague but also want to specify more than one cat, you can use something like 'some', 'all' or 'both'. We'll call this kind of word a `qadj`, which means *quantity adjective*. The more complex case is where we have an optional `qadj` followed by 'of' (a `qprep`), perhaps followed by something which specifies exactly how many you want, and possibly how many you expect there to be. This number checking is meaningful for sentences such as 'get the box' and 'get a box', which both work if there's only one box, but if there are two, then the first fails. I won't go into the details of that here as it gets messy, but it's in the final version of the syntax at the end of this chapter.

There are three kinds of <augment>: a <path> (which describes how to find the objects in question, eg. 'under the table'); an <exclusion> (which says what objects are to be rejected if they have certain properties, eg. 'but for the green cheese' – as opposed to <adjg>* which accepts them on the basis of their properties); and an <expath> (which does for <path>s what <exclusion> does for <adjg>s, as in 'which is not beneath the dome'). A <path> is just a preposition followed by another <ng>, that's easy. An <exclusion> is a 'negation preposition' such as 'without', 'excluding' or 'but', followed by an optional 'for', followed by a list of <ng>s (which we've already described and called an <objg>). The hardest, and probably the one least likely to be used, is <expath>, which again I shall include in the final version of the syntax but will not detail here.

So that's it! We've finished the informal summary of our grammar, now let's see it in its full, magnificent glory, in BNF.

6.10 A SYNTAX FOR COMMANDS

We now have a reasonable grammar for the subset of English which we will be using, and which (hopefully) is capable of parsing complex sentences. How exactly it's going to do that will be explained later on. The grammar is still not ideal, for example, there is no way to say something like 'stop doing a laugh' to terminate a 'laugh every 20 seconds' command, and a number of colloquialisms such as 'a couple of minutes' rather than 'a few minutes' aren't handled. It's not bad, though, and certainly better than what's available in most adventures currently on the market! Consider also that, compared with the grammars used in full-blown NL systems – which can have several *hundred* production rules – this one's a mere baby! Still, it's sufficient for our purposes. So here, then, is the full (type 2) grammar for commands likely to crop up in MUDS.

```
<sentence> ::= <actiong> <conjg>*
<actiong> ::= wadv wprep? <length>
              <conjg>? | <whenfirst> |
              <whensecond> | <action>
<conjg> ::= conj conj? <actiong>

<length> ::= <timea> | <timev>
<timea> ::= number? unit
<timev> ::= indobj wadj? unit

<whenfirst> ::= <wheng> conj? <wqual>?
                <action>
<whensecond> ::= <wqual>? <action>
                 <wheng>
```

```
<wheng> ::= <when> <length>
<wqual> ::= wverb indobj?
<when> ::= oadv | radv

<action> ::= <verbobjins> | <verbinsobj>
             | <insverbobj>
<verbobjins> ::= <vqg>* verb <vqg>
                 *<objins>?
<verbinsobj> ::= <vqg>* verb <vqg>
                 *<how>? <objg> <objg>?
                 <vqg>*
<insverbobj> ::= <vqg>* <how> <objg>
                 <vqg>* verb <vqg>
                 *<obj>?
<objins> ::= <objg> <vqg>* <ins>?
<ins> ::= <how> <objg> <vqg>*
<obj> ::= <objg> <vqg>*

<how> ::= prep | hprep? ptcple
<vqg> ::= <repeat> | adverb
<repeat> ::= tadverb | number tnoun

<objg> ::= <ng> <nconjg>*
<nconjg> ::= conj? <ng>
<ng> ::= string | <count>? <adjg>*
         <identity> <augment>?

<count> ::= indobj | qadj | <quantg>?
            <spec>
<quantg> ::= qadj qprep?
<spec> ::= <det> <predg>? | <predg>
<det> ::= padj | defobj
<predg> ::= number <pred>? | <pred>
            number?
<pred> ::= <restrict> <qprepg>?
<restrict> ::= superl | maxmin adj
<qprepg> ::= qprep <det>

<adjg> ::= adj conj*
<identity> ::= noun | pronoun | number
<augment> ::= <path> | <exclusion> |
              <expath>

<path> ::= prep <ng>
<exclusion> ::= nprep wprep? <objg>
<expath> ::= <which>? <what>

<which> ::= relpron pverb nadverb*
<what> ::= <det> <pred> <fromg> | <path>
           | <adjg>
```

```
<fromg> ::= qprep <fqg>
<fqg> ::= <det> number | pronoun
```

Since the above uses lots of terminals which you are unlikely to remember offhand (I don't even remember them all myself!), here are some example words for each of them. There are a few new classifications based on some of the definitions I glossed over:

```
wadv ::= wait | pause
wprep ::= for
conj ::= and | or | then
number ::= one | two | three | 1 | 2 | 3
unit ::= moment | seconds | bit | hours
         | minutes | while
indobj ::= a | an
wadj ::= few
wverb ::= do | execute | perform
oadv ::= after
radv ::= every
verb ::= go | get | drop | pick | shout
         | open | run
prep ::= with | at | to | from | on |
         under | carrying | below |
         inside
hprep ::= by
ptcple ::= employing | using | utilising
adverb ::= quickly | slowly | carefully
           | carelessly | on | up
tadverb ::= once | twice | thrice
tnoun ::= time | times
string ::= "hello there old son" | "why
           don't you just clear off?" |
           "where is the nearest public
           convenience?"
qadj ::= all | both | some | any
qprep ::= of
padj ::= my | your | his | her | its |
         their | our
defobj ::= the | this | that
superl ::= biggest | smallest | largest
           | greenest | fourth
maxmin ::= most | least | more | less
adj ::= big | red | heavy | shiny | human
        | valuable
noun ::= everything | treasures | men |
         woman | sack | tree | door
pronoun ::= it | him | her | them | me
nprep ::= without | excluding | except |
          but
```

```
relpron ::= which | who | that
pverb ::= is | are
nadverb ::= not
```

Our earlier 'test' sentence:

```
after 3 seconds, quickly open all three
orange boxes by using the largest of the
steel spikes in the rucksack, then knock
on all the doors except the biggest one
twice
```

now gives word assignments of:

```
oadv number unit adverb verb qadj number
adj noun hprep ptcple defobj superl
qprep defobj adj noun prep defobj noun
conj verb adverb qadj defobj noun nprep
defobj superl number tadverb
```

It doesn't make much sense like that if you just look at it, but we can check that it fits our syntax by doing a bottom-up parse on it. Looking at the stuff after the conj, I'll do such a parse of the second phrase of the sentence. To follow it, write out the word assignments at the bottom of a sheet of paper and draw the parse tree upwards from there, labelling each node as it's created. If you don't want to follow it, I don't blame you!

superl is a <restrict> is a <pred> is a <predg>.

defobj is a <det>, <det> <predg> is a <spec> is a <count>.

number is an <identity>, and <count> <identity> is a <ng> is an <objg>.

nprep followed by <objg> is an <exclusion>, and hence an <augment>.

qadj is a <quantg>, defobj is a <det> is a <spec>, and when preceded by a <quantg> is a <count>.

noun is an <identity>, and <count> <identity> <augment> is a <ng>, so is therefore an <objg>.

adverb is a <vqg>, as is a tadverb (via <repeat>).

An <objg> followed by a <vqg> is an <objins>, and verb

<vqg> <objins> is a <verbobjins>, and is thus an <action>, and so an <actiong>.

We could do the same sort of thing for the first part of the sentence, but it's much too long to include here. You might want to try it out yourself, but I suppose it's bad enough just following the process when it's already worked out *for* you! No wonder we want to write computer programs to do all this!

The inclusion of pronouns in the above syntax, by the way, is of dubious merit; it actually encourages people to use the wretched things! I put them in for completeness, but experience with MUD has shown that few people use them regularly. The problem is that mobiles and/or players keep arriving and fouling up the referent of the pronoun by superseding it with themselves. If a bunny rabbit arrived in a room, you'd want to be able to say 'get it', so it updates the 'it' pointer to itself. However, if I wanted to pick up a treasure chest and typed 'get it', then just before I hit the return a bunny rabbit hopped into the room , I could well end up holding a floppy-eared fluffy object instead of my loot, which someone else had by now removed. Even worse things can happen with pronouns like 'him' and 'her'. If I met some crazed low-level player with a long name and I wanted to demonstrate my disapproval by killing them, I could just type 'kill them'; it would be unfortunate if some super-powerful, god-like being materialised at the same moment and I ended up fighting them instead! The perils of a real-time game! However, in games which are not played in real-time, this problem will not arise.

Finally, it is worth noting that the above (huge) grammar is recursive. It is possible for <ng>s to go on indefinitely simply by putting prepositions between them. So 'the ball on the table underneath the tree in the orchard by the wall across the street next to the motorway outside the school containing . . . ' and so on, would be OK. It is just a highly detailed description indicating *which* ball you want. A shorter one would be 'the ball on the table'.

Prepositions are not only used this way, they are also used to separate object and instrument in a sentence: 'place the ball on the table'. This is the pp-attachment ambiguity I mentioned earlier – does 'burn the ball on the table' mean set fire to the ball which is at present on the table (as opposed to any other balls), or does it mean ignite the ball, and do it on the table (rather than anywhere else)? Unfortunately the recursion, coupled with a dual meaning for the prepositions, makes this problem insurmountable; the sentence genuinely *does* have two meanings, each as good as the other.

7
REAL-LIFE PARSERS

7.0 SLOTS FROM DERIVATION TREES

Given the grammar which was so laboriously constructed in the previous chapter, how might we do a shallow parse? Once we have the parse tree, it is a relatively simple matter to 'read off' the five components which we wish to return as our result, namely:

Delay
Action
Objects
Instruments
Repetitions

This is because they correspond to the subtrees beneath the nodes which represent their respective superior non-terminal symbols. So we can easily find the value for the delay by looking at the uppermost `<actiong>`'s 'when' components, and using some mindless, mechanistic process to come up with the number of seconds which must elapse before we evoke the action – and whether it is to be repeated or not. For example, this process might change 'a few minutes' into '3 minutes', and thence into '180 seconds'; 'a while' might translate into a random number between, say, 10 and 20 seconds. Whatever kind of non-terminal node we look at in the derivation tree, we'll always do the same thing for all nodes of that type. Extending this should get us our five sentential components.

It gets a bit more complex for things like the verb, of course, because you have to take into account the adverbs. Adverbs are modifiers to the verb, they fine-tune it so that its action will be performed in a certain way. This is implemented by having a table of `verb/adverb/newverb` triples somewhere. You take the set of adverbs from the structure, and look up each one on some property list associated with the word which the verb represents. Keep on going until you find a match. If you don't find one, then just ignore that adverb (they'll have said something either mundane, like 'climb the ladder normally', or just plain irrelevant, maybe 'climb the ladder thirstily').

Once you find a match for the verb and adverb, the third element of the triple gives a new verb into which the adverb 'changes' the original one. You can then take this new verb and scan the rest of the adverbs for it until, eventually, no further matches are found. In this way, a phrase like 'get the box quickly' would be transformed into 'snatch the box', because get + quickly = snatch. This technique works well for multiple applications, for example:

go + slowly = stroll
stroll + slowly = creep
creep + quickly = stroll.

If the new verb doesn't have a name, just invent one which people won't be able to type in, but which is otherwise just like a normal verb. So press + hard = hardpress might be used to check whether someone has pressed a button hard enough for it to function. In other words, it needs the presence of the adverb for the action to work.

The hardest kinds of sentential element to read off are objects and instruments. They both use the same algorithms for translating the derivation tree into its elementary form, as they are both obtained using identical BNF rules. However, there are several structural features which have to be retained, including the number of objects mentioned, whether this number must be exact or may be less than the number available to choose from, and what other objects must be examined in order to find this one ('get the scalp from the pouch'). What is required is a structure which we can assign to our object or instrument slot, and which may be arbitrarily large (because the path information references other objects, and will require that these other objects be stored in the same manner). That said, it's still not difficult to locate the objects using the parse tree, merely tedious.

We needn't, at this stage, go into the details of 'executing' the parse tree in this manner to obtain the summing-up details of the sentence (which we need to pass to the deep parse module), because it's fairly obvious how it's done if you look at it. It's lots and lots of pieces of almost identical code, which aren't of any use to anyone. The really hard part of the exercise is in constructing the derivation tree in the first place, starting with the rules of the grammar and the input string produced by the lexical analyser; it is to this topic that I shall devote most of this chapter.

7.1 FINITE STATE DIAGRAMS

The method used here relies on the *transition network*, more sophisticated versions of which are state-of-the-art in AI natural language work at the moment. I shall not be giving you chunks of programming language to look at, but attempt to convey the details in words so that it's easier to follow, and if you do want to write one, you can do it yourself without *too* much of a problem. First, however, I'd better go over the basics.

Transition Networks are a way of representing syntax graphically, in much the same way that Semantic Nets can be used to represent Frames (and vice-versa). Basic transition networks are called *Finite State Diagrams* (FSDs), and consists of a series of numbered nodes connected by terminal symbols from the BNF description. None of the rewrite rules are used, just the terminals. The rules are, however, encapsulated in the diagram. The usual example is for a simple noun group, where the BNF productions:

```
<ng> ::= <det> adj* noun
<det> ::= defobj | indobj
```

would correspond to the network in Figure 7.1 (`defobj` might be 'the', `indobj` might be 'a'). In Figure 7.1 we have two nodes, 'start' and 'end', and we need to find a route between them. There are three other nodes, 1, 2 and 3, and there are eight arcs, each marked with a terminal symbol from the BNF. We get from start to end by looking at the next thing on the input, and deciding in which direction to go on the basis of what nodes it could be. Given 'the small tin beaker' as our string, we'd start at 'start', see that the first word is a `defobj` ('the'), and go to node number 1. The next one is

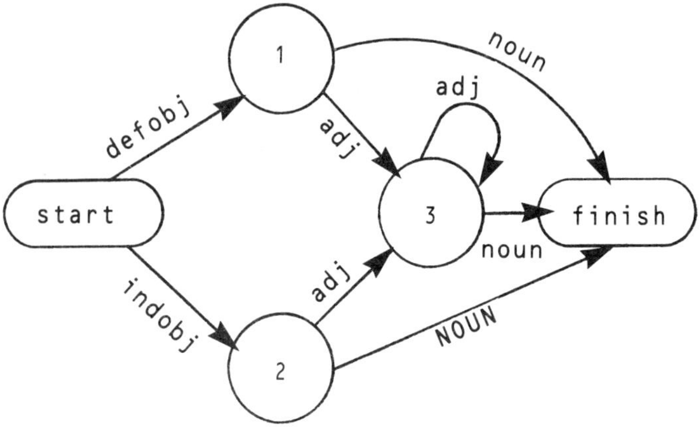

Note: The nodes in this network are also called *states*, and because there is always a finite number of them – even though our example grammar allows a sentence with an infinite number of consecutive adjectives – we get the *finite state diagram* name. I shall, however, carry on calling them *nodes* rather than states, to avoid confusion with the *world states* introduced previously in the Predicate Calculus.

Figure 7.1 Finite State Diagram

an `adj`, so we go to node 3. We stay there for the 'tin' because that's another `adj`, and finally 'beaker' is a `noun` which takes us on to the finish. All the words in the sentence have been used up, the sign that the parse worked correctly.

Now we could have problems with our FSD: for example, 'tin' is a noun as well as being an adjective, so when we're looking at the word 'tin' at node 3, we might decide it was a noun and go to the finish node prematurely instead of looping round back to 3 again. At this point we would find that the – supposedly parsed – phrase still contained unexamined words, so we'd have to backtrack to node 3 and make a different choice for the meaning of 'tin'. Similarly, if all the input consisted of was 'the small tin', and we had decided that 'tin' was an adjective instead of a noun, we'd still be at node 3 expecting a noun to take us on to the finish, but with no more words left; again, we'd have to backtrack and try alternative meanings of 'tin'. If we couldn't find any, we probably made a bad choice at the previous node in the network, and it would be necessary to backtrack to that point and try a different choice – and so on. If we get all the way back to the start, it was a dud.

This backtracking method is the most common way of traversing Transition Networks, and is very easy in languages such as PROLOG (which do it automatically). The alternative is *parallel processing*, which allows you try them all simultaneously, carrying on until finding the finish. Backtracking amounts to a *depth-first* search of the transition network, parallel processing is a *breadth-first* one.

It was not too easy to create the FSD from the BNF. Although I didn't actually describe *how* the network was constructed, I wrote out all the terminals, linked them together as indicated in the grammar, and expanded the non-terminals (<det> in our example) into the diagram. The process is much easier if we allow transitions between states *without* having to match against an input, by using 'empty' arcs. It's also easier to read and to program. It's not really the 'official' way to do it, though, since it can force backtracking even when the sentence is unambiguous; this is because empty arcs are always valid choices at nodes, and may be chosen at times when they really ought not to be. If you add an interpretation that empty arcs should always be tried last, you don't ever need to backtrack unless a word has several meanings, however. If there is no backtracking, it is possible to be more efficient in traversing the network, as I'll describe shortly.

The previous diagram, re-drawn using this 'null arcs are acceptable' convention, is given in Figure 7.2. It has been slightly optimised by combining pairs of nodes which are connected together only by empty arcs. Construction here was based on providing a node number for each 'gap' between symbols in the BNF production. In execution, transference between nodes is either automatic (along an unlabelled arc), or by matching against the next word in the input sentence (if it's of the right lexical type). This way of drawing transition networks is the one used by AI researchers (although sometimes they label the empty arcs with a 'jump' symbol); since this is the norm, I'll use this form from now on.

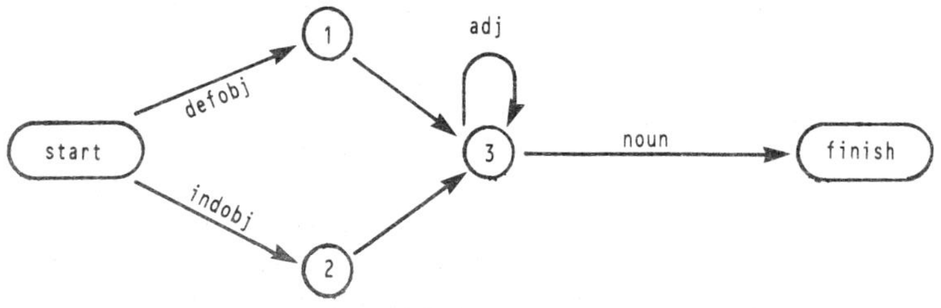

Figure 7.2 Finite State Diagram with Null Arcs

For non-terminal symbols, we just look at their expansion, write it out using the same algorithm, and then splice it into the main FSD, linking in the start and finish nodes at the appropriate spots. We have a problem in that we can't include the network for a non-terminal if its expansion involves recursion. Take the more complicated definition of a <ng>, which says as part of it that it is possible to follow the noun by a <path>, where a <path> is defined as a preposition (such as 'on') followed by another <ng>. We can't expand <ng> into the network as we're already in the process of trying to expand it! This is going to need a more sophisticated diagram . . . .

7.2 RECURSIVE TRANSITION NETWORKS

The straight FSD with no backtracking can be traversed by a type 3 grammar. This can be implemented very efficiently in most programming languages by a table look-up, which takes the node number and current input, and gives the node which should next be taken in the network. If you want some kind of recursion, ie. self-reference, though, an FSD is inadequate (and so is a type 3 grammar). A new kind of network is required to deal with it. This is the Recursive Transition Network (RTN). The name comes from the way transitions made from one state to the next may involve recursive transitions for different inputs. You can stop processing the current network, parse a bit more of the sentence with a sub-network, then return to where you left off. The recursion means you have to stack up pointers to where you were in one network when asked to traverse another one; this way, the number of states which may be active at any time is not fixed, you can recurse as often as you like. So if we had a string with an infinite number of <ng>s, there would be an infinite number of states in action, so it's non-finite (unlike a FSM, which of course is!). Hence, not all RTNs are FSMs (although all FSMs are RTNs).

An RTN looks like a normal FSM except that it doesn't have to be restricted to terminals, it may include non-terminals as well. Figure 7.3 shows an RTN for the following BNF definitions:

```
<ng> ::= <det>? adj* noun <path>?
<det> ::= defobj | indobj
<path> ::= prep <ng>
```

So how do you parse using an RTN? Assume that you have already written the lexical analyser and it has looked up the various words and found their corresponding types. It tells you that 'tin', for example, is both a noun and an adjective. These terminal symbols will become the input string presented to the RTN. Also assume that you have some data structure (maybe a table of some kind) to represent the RTN. Starting at the 'start' node of the `sentence` network, make a choice between the alternative matches between word class and arc class. The same kind of choices are available at any node, so let us consider what to do in general. Look at the choices on the arcs, select the ones which either match the input or are non-terminals, and pick one of them: if it is a non-terminal symbol, then push onto a stack the pointer to 'where you are at the moment', then reset it to the start node of the new network; if it is a terminal symbol, then if the input could be of that type, move to the node indicated in that direction (and move along to the next word in the input string, too); if it's an unlabelled arc, just move to the next node and do nothing; if there are no arcs leaving the node then it is a 'finish' state, so 'pop' the previous pointer you have on the stack, and move back to that network and to the pointed-at node.

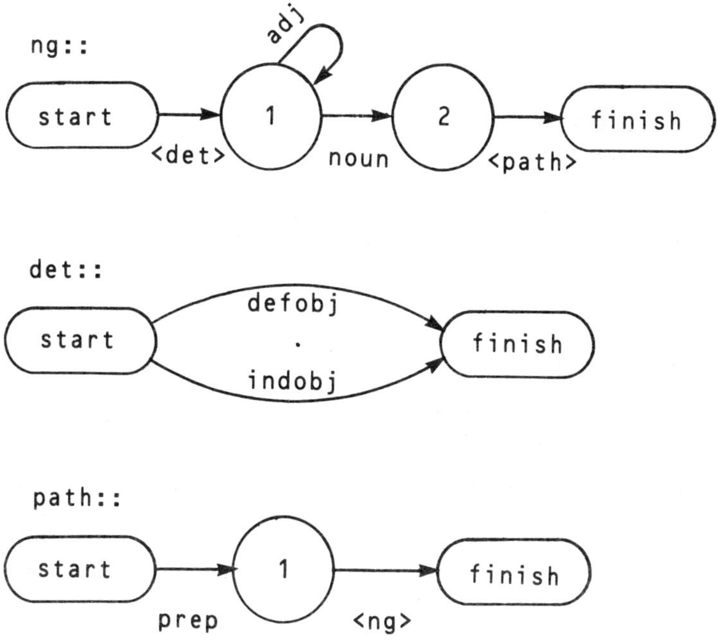

Figure 7.3 Recursive Transition Network

If there is nothing on the stack to pop, then you've reached the end of the sentence and it is time to check that there are no words left on the input: if there aren't then you've finished; otherwise you made a bad choice somewhere and will have to backtrack.

There are many ways to backtrack, the simplest being *chronological backtracking*, which means you go back to the choice you made last and try another alternative. This is a depth-first method, and can be quite slow for fairly long sentences which go wrong early on. The easiest way to write it is to put all your RTN-traversing actions into a function which comes up true or false. If it returns true, then the parse beyond this point was successful, so the parse including this point was also successful, so just return true from here. If it returned false, then the parse beyond here failed, so try your next choice (and if there aren't any, fail at this node too).

For the start node in the `<ng>` above you would have program instructions to the effect of:

- If I can parse a determiner, then if I can parse from state 1 onwards then return true; if I can parse from state 1 onwards anyway then return true; otherwise, return false

Trying to parse non-terminals like `<det>`, this algorithm will recursively try to parse the appropriate subnetwork starting at its own 'start'. When it finishes, then it will return to where it was invoked, and control will be back with the node that called it.

The above is an operational description at a level of detail sufficient to enable enthusiastic readers to go off and write their own RTN parsers in whatever language they like. It's fairly common-sense, but there are other ways to do it which you might care to invent for yourself. If you want to try it out, write a small grammar with only a tiny number of productions, and see how you get on. Then you can try it on the syntax developed in the previous chapter, or perhaps on some modification to it which packs an even bigger punch!

The process described above is not exactly a parser, only what is called a *recogniser*. That means that you can give it an input string and it will be able to tell you whether it is a valid sentence in the grammar or not, maybe even what parts of speech are associated with each word, to iron out ambiguities. However, there is no structure involved and to obtain one it is not enough simply to return a true value when a recursive call succeeds, the parser must have a way of building up a data structure to represent the derivation tree. Hence, it ought also to return (in some accessible place) the tree below the point where it was called.

By tree, I mean a pointer to some representation of the parse tree. This would probably be best done by creating records from a suitable dynamic storage mechanism such as a *heap*. The records would need a *type* field, to say what kind of node the record denotes and, if it was a non-terminal node, a list of subtrees which were created by parsing the right-hand side of the augmented BNF production. What results from this can be sketched diagramatically, and looks exactly like the kind of derivation tree diagram which appeared in Chapter 6. You can only produce a data structure which is isomorphic to the grammar rules used when the grammar is phrase-structure, that is a type 1 or 2 grammar. Although these are desirable for this rule-to-structure mapping feature, they are not powerful enough to cope with absolutely anything which may be thrown at them, since they cannot handle type 0 grammars. If you are in a position to define the grammar of the language (as you would be when designing a programming language), then phrase-structure is definitely the version to go for. Most modern programming languages can be parsed this way, obviating the need for back-tracking.

7.3 AUGMENTED TRANSITION NETWORKS

RTNs are perfectly suitable for parsing as far as MUDs are concerned, and certainly a good deal better than systems used in most current adventure games. I ought to point out, however, that although this may seem quite sophisticated to non-AI people, it barely scratches the surface of what is routinely achieved in the Natural Language field. NL theorists have vastly more powerful systems at their fingertips, but are often not very concerned with such mundane matters as applications projects. Some of the big programs can take several minutes to parse a sentence; this doesn't mean they're of no use, they help a great deal with understanding deeper issues relating to intelligence. What it does mean is that they're not practical. People who want real-time programs generally need to sacrifice some of the strong points to achieve the speed required, but even then these programs are many orders of magnitude more powerful than the RTN I have described here. This mechanism will seem rather rudimentary to NL researchers, as they have quite a number of quicker and more powerful algorithms at their disposal, and far better grammars than the one which I developed here. This enormous gap in expertise is one of the major reasons why people in the games industry would do well to wake up to AI.

If AI researchers spent more time designing parsers which would satisfy the everyday need to represent commands (which is how most human-to-computer instructions would be phrased) rather than mere facts ('The girl on the red bus was wanted in several countries by the police.') and queries ('Was the fire engine trying to get to the fire?'), then perhaps the experience of real, live people trying to use their system might give fresh insights into their work. A clearer understanding of the term 'semantics', which has not as yet been given a truly persuasive interpretation in AI, would certainly be on the cards and, indeed, any serious delving into the area from a NL point of view would find the topic almost begging for treatment.

Although I have described the process of parsing using an RTN, these are not in common use in the important NL systems around today. This is because RTNs are not powerful enough to parse type 0 grammars, and many of the grammars for those subsets of English which need to be parsed are written in a type 0 form. If we want to parse these grammars using a Transition Network regime, we need something known as *Augmented Transition Networks* (ATNs).

ATNs are RTNs, but, as the name implies, they are augmented in certain ways. Essentially, they have three extra features which aren't possessed by RTNs, and which make a lot of linguistic problems much easier to deal with.

I won't describe how to write an ATN in detail, since it's a bit of a culture shock if you've only just learned about RTNs. Also, ATNs will parse 'all the way' so that you should be able to make them *do* things when they've finished. The shallow parse which we require does not need to go into this kind of depth – that's what the deep parse is for! So although I shall look at ATNs, because they're an important alternative, I won't give much in the way of detail that would enable you to write one.

The first ATN extra is a set of registers, which are used to do things like store the partially formed derivation trees when 'expanding' a non-terminal node into a subtree. Apart from other things, this means that if perfectly reasonable parses were made for sections of the input string and the rest of the parse failed, then the results of the good parse can be saved and used again when an earlier, incorrect choice-point is corrected and they come to be parsed again. For example, if the sentence was 'the sheep in the small meadow by the river was small', then an RTN might assume that 'sheep' were plural first, get as far as 'was', and fail on attempting to match against the noun. Backtracking as far as 'sheep' would mean a new choice could be tried, to make it parse the word as a singular noun. This would then succeed, and all would be well. However, the section 'in the small meadow by the river' has been parsed twice – in exactly the same way each time (once when sheep was assumed to be singular, and then a second time for the plural case). Saving derivation trees in global registers means that work need not be repeated unnecessarily.

The registers can also be used for things like stacking up pronouns so that correct interpretations of words such as 'it' may be found. As registers are associated with each network in the ATN, when a call to parse a non-terminal group is made then the registers for the current net must be saved, and restored when control is returned to that net from below.

The next addition which makes ATNs what they are is associating functions or actions with arcs. These actions are executed when the arc is taken, and usually they modify the registers in some way. The main ones set registers to some value, but others can access the registers in the networks above or below this one in the hierarchy of what-has-called-what. This makes sense, for example if there is no noun in the current network to which 'it' could refer, then maybe there's one on the network above. 'Get the box and weigh it' has the 'it' at the same level as 'the box', whereas 'Get the box and weigh the key in the drawer in it' doesn't.

The main point of these registers is that arbitrary tests may also be associated with each arc in the network. These tests must be passed if the arc is to be taken, so they act as 'preconditions'. Some of the tests may be context-free, including actions like looking at word endings to see whether they are appropriate; others will be context-sensitive, looking at the register values.

This kind of test can speed up things considerably. For example, if a register were set to be 'plural', then tests could be put on noun arcs to ensure that singular nouns didn't get through. Although this plural/singular distinction can be made by using different syntactic non-terminal symbols, one set for plural and one for singular, the register test way avoids duplicating all the common sections of the grammar involved, only checking on the necessary verb plurality agreement. Hence in the phrase 'the sheep in the small meadow by the river was small', it would parse as far as 'was', and then check that 'sheep' was singular before allowing the parse to proceed. Since 'sheep' can be both singular or plural, it would pass the test. This way keeps all the options open. Without registers, if the sheep were marked as being plural, then 'was' would make the parser backtrack all the way to 'sheep', and the intervening section might well have to be repeated.

The difference between ATNs and RTNs is surprisingly small so that most of the advantages (and disadvantages) of ATNs apply to RTNs. ATNs are very flexible, and can be used to implement most grammars quite easily. There are even programs which, given a suitable syntax, will write ATNs for you. ATNs can run quickly and efficiently, and work on fairly complicated examples. Apart from relatively mundane ones concerning girls on red buses being wanted by police, they can also cope with less palatable problems. The following sets of progressively obscure sentences which crop up in the ATN literature will demonstrate this:

> The girl screamed.
> The girl the man kissed screamed.
> The girl the man the mugger robbed kissed screamed.
> I called up my neighbour.
> I called my neighbour up.
> I called my neighbour in the town where I used to live before financial problems forced me to move to Chicago last month up.

ATNs can generate any kind of sentence, as they have type 0 power. They can represent the grammar rules efficiently, and can cover a lot of generalities of languages. The main reason for their widespread use, though, is because they run like the wind compared to most other parsing strategies.

ATNs are not perfect, however. They can get terribly confused register-wise when dealing with long sentences. They also rely heavily on syntax, so that meaningful yet ungrammatical or mis-spelled input is a problem ('feed the cat with th mouse'). The very latest high-powered grammars are written in a kind of modified BNF formalism, which includes 'meta-rules' to say what kind of BNF production rules are currently appropriate. Trying to put this into an ATN would drive you up the wall! However, ATNs are particularly good at handling certain other popular kinds of grammar such as *transformational grammars* (TG). These are more all-embracing than phrase-structure grammars, but they lose the correspondence between rules and derivation tree.

7.4 OTHER WAYS TO PARSE

Other ways to parse sentences exist, and as with most AI systems they're good at some things, hopeless at others. Simple pattern matching, which is employed in ELIZA and PARRY, is very good if you want a superficial yet flexible system, which won't ever crash on inputs. For languages which over-use words and give them many meanings, though, more precise grammars may be needed to make the fine distinctions necessary to choose between alternatives.

For example, the meta-rule (rules about rules) approach was brought in for two reasons. The theoretical one was to make it easier to write shorter grammars and provide the author with more control. The practical one was because of a 'combinatorial explosion'. This means that the more features you add to your system, the longer it takes to parse them. The time rises exponentially with the number of extras added and with the length of the sentences input. That said, even using the most efficient kind of parser currently in favour, the *chart parser*, ten-word sentences can take minutes to parse if the grammar is large enough.

These sophisticated grammars, the commonest variation of which are *Generalised Phrase-Structure Grammars* (GPSG), can take in an immense number of production rules, and present a formidable vocabulary. Rules of the form 'if you have a production which looks like this, then you can also have one which looks like this' tend to generate new rules, and hence they have the meta-rule label. They are particularly good at making it easier to write productions for different tenses, but they also have other uses, not least of which involves taking the tedium out of writing rules for plurality agreements (the plural form is only a slight modification to the singular case). Putting this kind of strength into an ATN would mean sentences would take orders of magnitude longer to parse.

Some other specialised grammars are specially constructed so that when you've written them, you end up with a parser. In particular, *Definite Clause Grammars* (DCGs) are arranged such that the rules look like pieces of PROLOG, and you can read them in and run them on your PROLOG interpreter. Most good books on PROLOG will give you a DCG as an example, so if you do have PROLOG available, it is worth having a good look at the documentation provided.

The parsers I've mentioned so far are all *non-deterministic*. That means they occasionally make the wrong choice when trying out alternatives, and have to backtrack. A *deterministic* parser never backtracks; instead, it has a certain number of symbols which it can examine in advance. This is a kind of look-ahead mechanism, and normally the buffer in which symbols are stored before processing is two or three long. Deterministic parsers have a lot going for them in theory, but haven't yet been proven to any great extent in practice. They certainly don't cope too well with sentences where large gaps appear between related words ('I produced with a flourish so swift that it caused m' lady to stop eating in her awe my sword.').

A good deal of attention these days has been focussed on so-called *semantic grammar parsers*. The idea here is that instead of using the normal way to describe words, in terms of `<noun>`s and `<verb>`s and the like, they are a classification based on the application domain. So for a cookery program, classes such as `<ingredient>`, `<utensil>` and `<preparation>` might be appropriate, for things like salt/water/asparagus, knife/peeler/mixer, and boil/mince/saute.

The advantage with these systems is that taking this approach you can often build up a normal PSG parser, which comes down to standard word types. Also, it's easier to 'interpret' the data structure you have at the end: the meaningful parts are nodes in the tree, with their subtrees where necessary. These can be related to primitive, executable, actions. So a `<preparation>` of 'cut', when actually executed, will run a piece code which actually 'does' the cutting in the world model, ie. update it so the new state is such that the cut has been made.

If desired, the execution of primitives can be partitioned off from the first phase of the parse. It can even take place on a separate machine. In other grammars, more work may need to be done to transform the structure into something which can be executed (except for DCGs, which will run directly, and can have actions coded into them).

One example of such a semantic grammar is the *case grammar*. Here, each noun phrase is related to the verb in some semantically relevant syntactic way. So 'Mildred cut the paper with scissors and made a hat' would say things like the `<agent>` was 'Mildred', the `<object>` was 'paper', the `<instrument>` was 'scissors', and the `<result>` was the 'hat'. In the initial formalisation, which was made in the late 1960s, there were around eight of these fairly general cases, although alternative sets have been proposed since then with more of them (or less).

If this is starting to look familiar, so it should. This kind of semantic grammar is the one I have been outlining for our adventure game parser. By starting off with the categories required, we built up the syntax of a PSG which we could parse with an RTN, and we can read the corresponding slots off from the resulting derivation tree. If we think of implementational matters for moment, then in a MUD, the whole of the process described so far could be done on the user's home microcomputer. Now we need to tie the slots onto some executable code, which in a MUD means altering the world ('eat potato' makes the potato disappear), and that certainly wouldn't be done on the user's machine for all manner of reasons related to the operating system; no-one can change the world model at the same time as someone else, rather in the same way that you can't have two people writing to the same file in a normal timesharing computer. So, in writing a MUD, the database update part could be put on a separate machine. This architectural consideration, between the parts of MUDs which can be done in parallel (the shallow parses on the players' own machines) and the part which can't (the deep parse on the host computer) played a key role in my decision to partition the system into the separate shallow and deep parse phases which I have developed in this book.

7.5 THE DEEP PARSE

The purpose of the deep parse is to find the relevant code to execute, given a set of slot values. If two of the slots were `[destroy, ball]`, for example, then the appropriate action might be to remove the ball from the database. When it comes to dealing with questions, some information must be obtained and returned to the user (`[where, crayon]` might send back the reply 'in the desk').

The nature of primitive operators is a bone of contention among AI folk. The early work centred around a system called *conceptual dependency* (CD), which was initially quite popular but which has since been superseded by more sophisticated schemes. Nevertheless it sparked off much research including the work on scripts discussed earlier. The basic idea remains the same, namely that you have some collection of hardwired actions, which are held to be understood by everyone. You take your slots and map them into these primitives to form a structure, and this provides the 'meaning' of the sentence. For executable commands, the nodes in this structure would have various small programs associated with them, and these would be run in some order.

The number of primitives can be quite small – the total settled on for conceptual dependency was around fourteen – and these are supposed to be language-independent. That means that if you take a sentence in English and its translation in Finnish, they would both reduce to the same structure in CD. So the primitives act as a kind of 'inter-lingua', the hope being that the deep structure they provide will correspond in some way to the structures inside the head of a bilingual person.

Another advantage of the shallow/deep distinction is that the shallow parse can be honed for a particular language, whereas the deep parse is completely language independent. From an adventure game point of view, this means that if you have shallow parsers for English, Russian, Portuguese and so on, then they can all use the same deep parse. A good way to sell lots of programs abroad with very little extra work, provided that it has been set up appropriately.

So how does the deep parse proceed? Essentially, it's just a matching operation. The five slots act as a *template*, and are matched in sequence against sets of *patterns*, or production rules. When the pattern matches, an associated piece of code is run. These pattern/code units are called *Case Frames* and the template elements are called *slots* because they really are slots, in the Frame sense of the word.

The matching between the template and the Case Frames will not be a straight equality comparison, it will involve a hierarchy of terms. If it is the case that setting fire to a piece of paper destroys it, setting fire to a piece of cloth destroys it, as does setting fire to tables, petrol cans, pigeons, pagodas, venetian blinds and a host of other things, then it would be silly to have different cases for each possible object, all with identical actions associated with them. It would make much more sense to state beforehand that 'all paper, cloth, tables, petrol cans, etc. are combustible'. Now you can say that when trying to burn any object, a check should first be made to see whether it has a combustible property and, if it has, then destroy it – otherwise don't. It may be even better if you say that all these objects are of the class 'combustible', so all pieces of paper are also combustibles. This is a good use for the 'a kind of' hierarchy, we can say that you can burn anything which is `ako` combustible. So maybe roses are a kind of flower, flowers are a kind of plant, and plants are a kind of combustible, and therefore roses are combustible.

So the template matching will be hierarchically-based. The most specific matches should be tried first and, if they fail, they ought to be covered by more general, catch-all Frames. Many common actions tried by the user will be accounted for by these fairly high-level templates, so if they try to chop down a tree with anything other than an axe, the `[chop, tree, axe]` template will fail to match (ignoring the other slots for the moment), but `[chop, tree, object]` will match, and might possibly offer the advice that 'using an axe could perhaps produce the desired result'.

7.6 UNIFICATION AND INSTANTIATION

There is a problem in that in order to do something in the code part of the Case Frame, the object which is to be affected must first be discovered. It is surprisingly difficult to determine which object players mean. If a player says 'kill the rat', they will normally mean the rat which is in the same room as them. If they say 'where is the rat', then the entire universe must be searched to find a matching object so that its location can be revealed. In general, actions will require that the object be either held by the player or present in the room; if not then they will not work. If you want an object from somewhere else, perhaps a bag, then you must say so. The bag can be found by looking in the player's room, and the object can be found by looking in the bag. This is the 'path' information which becomes associated with objects when they're read off the derivation tree.

What we have here is an example of *unification* which, in its most general form, works as follows. Let's start with two lists, each consisting of objects (shown in lower case) and/or variables (upper case). Such lists are shown here using the PROLOG convention of using square brackets. Say the lists were `[A, b, c, d]` and `[a, b, c, D]`. To unify two lists, they must be of the same length. You *walk* the two lists simultaneously, considering each element in turn, comparing them with their opposites in the other list. If the element is a variable, then it will match against anything. If it is an object (usually called an *atom* in this context), then it will match against either a variable or an identical atom. If it is itself a list, it will match with another list if they both can be unified. Unification fails if you try to match non-identical atoms, non-unifiable lists, or lists against atoms.

That's not the whole story, because when you match a variable against something, it becomes *bound* to that value. So if I matched `A` against `a`, then `A` would be replaced by a wherever it occurred in the rest of the lists. It might as well *be* a, from then onwards. That means it wouldn't match against `b`, `[a]`, `aa`, or any other non-variable except `a`.

Another important point is that if you unify two variables, they then become one variable. So unifying `A` with `B` and then `B` with `c` would make `A` be `c`, too. You can easily follow this by just replacing all occurrences of the second variable by the first. It is not necessary to have a list to perform a unification: if you wanted to unify `A` and `b` then you could do so, you wouldn't have to put it as `[A]` and `[b]`. It is couched in list terms here because matching a template with a Case Frame looks just the same as unifying two lists.

In the above example, then, if you unify `[A, b, C, d]` with `[a, b, c, D]`, you get `A=a`, `C=c`, and `D=d`. They're both lists, so we just unify the elements in turn. `A` unifies with `a`, `b` unifies with `b`, `C` with `c` and `d` with `D`. The normal way to write these, as I have done here, is to give the bindings of the variables. Here are a few more examples you might like to work through yourself. Unification of:

`[A, B, A]` *with* `[B, c, D]`
gives: `A=c, B=c, D=c`

`[A, b, C, D]` *with* `[d, D, C, C]`
gives: `A=d, D=b, C=b`

`[[A, b, C], D, C]` *with* `[D, [a, C, C], E]`
gives: `A=a, C=b, D=[a, b, b], E=b`

The following don't unify for one reason or another:

`[A, B, C, D, A]` *with* `[b, D, B, a, C]`

`[A, B, C]` *with* `[A, b, A, D]`

`[A, b, C, D]` *with* `[a, a, d, c]`

This next one also fails, because the variable `A` occurs in the list with which it is to be unified:

`[[A, b, c], b, A]` *with* `[D, B, D]`

When you replace a variable with an atom or list, the process is called *instantiation*. Unifying `[A, A, B, D]` with `[D, d, B, A]` works as follows:

`A` binds to `D`, so replace all `D`s with `A`s (`[A, A, B, A]` and `[A, d, B, A]`)

`A` instantiates to `d` so replace all `A`s with `d`s (`[d, d, B, d]` and `[d, d, B, d]`)

`B` binds to itself and `d` matches against `d`

`A` is instantiated to `d`, `D` is bound to `A` so it is also instantiated to `d`, and `B` remains uninstantiated.

Unification works 'both ways'; that is, if you were unifying two lists then either of them could instantiate parts of the other. If you were to use unification to match formal and actual parameters in a procedure call in a normal programming language, then that would be a special case where the first list was all instantiated. If you used call-by-reference or call-by-name, then you could change the variables from within the subroutine; that would be like instantiating them for use later on in the main program. In PROLOG it's even easier, because unification is the *only* way to pass parameters and return results from functions!

With our Case Frame matches, we will usually be trying to compare two lists: the first will normally be instantiated to the object we wish to find, and the second won't. So if you gave a command with a corresponding template of [poke, cat] then it would match against the Case Frame [hit, animal], and instantiate hit=poke and animal=cat. If you asked [where, cat, room] it would match against [where, object, location], and instantiate location=cellar from within the body of the Case Frame (assuming that's where the cat was hiding). So the room variable would also be instantiated to the whereabouts of the cat as it is unified with location, thus receiving data back from the Case Frame.

The unification is slightly different from the norm here, because it is hierarchical. Unlike basic unification, where an atom will match any variable, here we only want them to match variables if they're the right type. So whereas unifying [cat, fiddle] with [drink, sunlight] is normally valid, we want to restrict matching to situations where the atom is ako the variable (or, for two variables, one is ako the other). Apart from that, the unifications we have to do are pretty straightforward.

Because unification is built in to PROLOG, a lot of this would be very easily implemented in that language. It is beyond the scope of this book to discuss the use of specific AI (or any other) languages, but if you do have a micro for which some form of PROLOG is available, then it will be well worth your while buying a copy if you're thinking of writing your own deep parser. You probably wouldn't want to program an entire game in it, but you'd certainly see the kind of features you'd have to mimic in any system you did write, and you'd have the bonus of being able to test your algorithms out in a friendly, co-operative environment.

7.7 REPRESENTING ACTIONS

We are now, at last, in a position to come up with some kind of representation for the actions themselves. We have already invented a schema for objects earlier in this book (the Wizard's Study), but actions have always been put off. Now is the time to say something concrete about them. I won't be as precise as I was for objects, however, because, as we shall see, so long as the actions obey certain criteria, their general format doesn't really matter.

Actions amount to functions, which act on the database. You can think of them as ordinary subroutines in a conventional programming language. If we look at some of our five slots, delay is the time we wait before we carry out the action, and repeat is the number of times we wish to do it. These aren't strictly necessary when unifying the template with the Case Frame, because they do the same set of things for whatever action you have. Hence, I won't bother defining them in the action formalism, as they'll always be the same and can be assumed.

So actions depend on the other three slots. These will be the action itself, and maybe an object, maybe also an instrument. Some actions won't need either one or both of these, for example a 'sneeze' command doesn't beg the question 'sneeze *what*?', unlike 'push' and 'cut'. These actions can have as their second and third slots some top-level variable which will match anything, and which they will ignore. Again, if they are going to be ignored, we don't need them here and I will use the syntactic convention that if only one or two slots are given, the remaining slots default to unique but unused variables.

So the Case Frame will have four slots. The first three will be for `verb`, `object` and `instrument`, and the fourth will be for the `body` of the Frame. This body will consist of other Frames, in some kind of a tree structure. From here onwards, the main thing to remember is that we're now designing a language. It can be as sophisticated as we like, with loops, conditionals, compound data structures, functions which can return functions, indeed whatever we feel capable of implementing. However, it is very likely that we will want to be able to call upon other Case Frame actions. Say we wanted to arrange things so that if you let go of a bell, the system replied 'now you've dropped a clanger'. The Case Frame would have `[drop, bell]` as its first two slots, and its body would have some output statement, followed by, well, by what? Really, since from here onwards it's just the same as [drop object], we ought to be able to call that Case Frame. Hence, it's a good idea to keep working with Frames as our representation, then we can slip in other Case Frames when we want to use 'subroutines'.

So the body will consist of *procedure calls*, which are other case Frames, and of an assortment of primitive functions. These primitives will act like built-in Case Frames, with their body being a piece of code somewhere. So if we had a branching instruction, `->`, it would have three slots. It would look at the first, execute it, and on the basis of whether this returned true or false, it would select the second or third slot and execute that. It's as if there were an interpreter – call it `eval` as LISP does – which takes a Frame, matches it against a Case Frame, and executes the `body` slot of it by calling `eval` on it. If the function is one that `eval` knows about (said to be *hardwired* into `eval`) then it can handle it directly. Otherwise, it will keep on going recursively until it comes across a primitive instruction it *can* evaluate.

What should these instructions be? This is up to you, the programmer. In the main, they will be Frame-manipulation routines, which change slot values, test them, and create new slots. There will also be some input/output routines, and other built-in predicates to handle communication, errors, and the like. MUD has about eighty of these, which range from the simple 'add 1 to the value in the slot' to the more complicated 'destroy the object and teleport the player to this room' variations. Really a lot of these are next to useless, but a small subset is certain to be needed. Arithmetic, for example, is rather essential! The best way to write this is to think of your own favourite language and model it on that. Unfortunately, 'how to write interpreters' is a subject which fills volumes all by itself and is well beyond our brief here.

There are also some basic routines which almost every adventure must have. These include the obvious `help`, `get`, `drop`, `quit`, `kill`, `move`, `inventory`, and `look`, but also the more obscure ones like `log` (the game in a file) and `save` (the game for later). With MUDS, you have a whole host of new commands which would be common to all multi-player games. These include `who` (is playing), `tell` (a player some message), `give`, `steal`, `follow`, `help`, `hours` (the game is open) and `kiss` (or whatever!). If you have some all-powerful beings, like MUD's wizards and witches, then you will need even more commands along the lines of `snoop` (on another player's screen), `invisible`, `enchant` (change your character attributes – commonly known as a *frig*), and `fod` (Finger Of Death!').

With these actions likely to occur in any adventure, it might be a good idea to build in some features for them. Rather than spend time interpreting a bundle of Frames, which simulate a `get` themselves by looking up slot values for the object and player, making sure the getter isn't carrying too much, checking that the object isn't nailed down or too heavy, and so on, it might be better if such common commands could be represented by a primitive action which did all the necessary computations in a proper programming language. As long as it never needed to access any other Case Frames, this would be fine. MUD does it, of course, and has almost one hundred such built-in primitives. This is probably too many, and some of them would be better off written out in full in a library of standard commands, as they would not all be required by the other games which run on the same interpreter.

So the representation for actions, then, is a long list – or table – of Case Frames. These Frames have a `body` slot, which is a pointer to another collection of Frames in a nice, neat tree structure, which can, in turn, be evaluated. When a command is given, it is unified in turn with each of the slots until it matches one, and then that slot's body is interpreted. This arrangement looks rather like that for a normal, interpreted programming language, and it is: but it is just as effective in a programming language developed for writing adventure games.

7.8 ACTION-CENTRED vs OBJECT-CENTRED

The way I have described things is normally considered *action-centred*, which means that the actions are the important bits. Many of the more professional adventures around, such as ZORK, use an *object-centred* philosophy, where objects are more important. The difference can be seen by comparing ways to think about some simple action such as kicking, applied to a simple object, such as a ball. In an action-centred world, you formulate this as 'it is a property of kick that when you apply it to a ball, the ball moves'. Object-centred, it comes out as 'it is a property of balls that if you kick them, they move'.

In action-centred systems, such as MUD, the action holds the key and you look up objects on its case Frame, match them, and execute the `body`. In the object-centred convention, you take the object, look up the action on its list of 'possible actions which can affect it', and interpret the associated `body` there. This works fine, and for many people it is more intuitive than the action-centred regime. However, it can get very confusing for sentences which have instruments as well as objects.

In the sentence 'light the fuel with the candle', is it a property of the fuel that when you light it with a (lit) candle it explodes, or is it a property of the candle that if it is lit then when you light fuel with it the fuel explodes? Or is it a property of both? What if there are other things you can light with candles that ignite but don't explode? What about other ways to explode fuel without using candles?

Action-centred languages don't have this problem, because there's never more than one `verb` in a sentence. It just happens that's a feature of natural languages. It's a cinch to say it's a property of the verb 'light' that when you do it with a lit candle to some fuel, the fuel explodes. It fits in quite naturally.

The whole debate about whether to go action-centred or object-centred came to light recently when I became involved in a discussion with a group at Xerox PARC (Palo Alto Research Centre), via the electronic mailing network. They are a fairly high-powered bunch (Don Woods, who worked on the original ADVENTURE, is there, but wasn't one of the group I was talking to), working on a game called YAFA ('Yet Another Fantasy Adventure'). As YAFA is object-centred and MUD isn't, we both had difficulty in understanding why the other hadn't used our choice of formalism. After a fast and furious exchange, they decided to incorporate some measure of action-centredness into YAFA to cover the awkward cases, but held out against going the whole way. The final agreement we came to was that 'action-centred' is a misnomer, and what we really have here is a 'verb-centred' language, where the 'verb' is just an object in an object-centred language. Who says the age of diplomacy is long since gone?

8

MORE AI

8.0 PLANNING

This final chapter gives a brief description of some of the other subfields of Artificial Intelligence relevant to computer games and vice versa. These are not detailed descriptions, only enough to give an overview of each such area and to make some suggestions as to how they could be fitted into an adventure game.

The first of these topics is *planning*. The basic task here is, on the face of it, quite simple. Given an initial state of the world, and some actions which can be executed to change one world state into some other, then produce a sequence of actions such that when they are executed in turn they get you from this initial state to some final, goal state.

Planning is very, very difficult, however, because the number of ways in which you can combine simple actions is so large that a straightforward search would be hopeless in all but the most trivial domains. If a robot hand could pick up objects and put them down in different places, and you wanted it to build up a stack of objects (toy blocks is the usual example), then there are many options available to it. Say it wanted to pick up one block but couldn't because it had another on top of it. It has to move the top one away somewhere. But where? The robot has a `[move, object, location]` action, and can only instantiate the first two slots. It needs to instantiate the location (the place to which it should move the offending block), so that it can pick up the one underneath. But there is an infinite number of places where the robot could put it! It might instantiate `location` to Kabul, and then trundle off on its little wheels to Afghanistan to dispose of the block, then return to its home to pick up the one it wanted originally and carry on with its task!

Also, it may try a few irrelevant actions. It might want to put block A on block B, and spend the first two hundred hours of its time messing about with blocks C and D, before finally grabbing A and dropping it on B. The plan it has produced certainly works, but it isn't approaching optimal!

So there has to be some sensible mechanism to stop it from making stupid moves. With simple domains, like the 'blocks world' this is done by building a *scheduler* – a program which looks at the possible ways of combining the base-level movement actions, selecting only the most likely looking ones. In this case, actions not involving the block you were thinking of moving would be ignored until they were absolutely necessary (you may need to move a different block to make room for some particular one upon which you were focussing your attention). This process of selecting which of many possibilities to apply is called *conflict resolution*. Conflict resolution rules are built in to the scheduler, *hardwired*. Another name for these ad-hoc rules (often used by the especially trendy) is *heuristics*.

In simple domains it's usually easy to decide what to do in a particular situation. However, in more complex ones you may have to choose which of many conflict resolution rules to apply! Consider the decision whether to forward-run or backward-run. If you forward-run, you look at the current state and try to work out a way of getting it closer to the goal state. You do this by predicting the state you would get after executing some action, and then comparing this with what you want; if you're not there try and to forward-run until you are. Backward-running is where you work back from the goal state, by looking for actions which you could have applied to get you to the goal state, and then trying to reach a situation where these actions may be applied.

So to build a stack of blocks with a robot arm, you would forward-run by thinking, 'hmm, if I move this to here, then what will I be able to do?' and backward-run with 'hmm, I only need to move this to here to do it, so how do I set things up to allow that move?'. If you simply pick one or other other of these strategies, then your system isn't very flexible. Besides, in some cases one of them may come to a conclusion very much quicker than the other. So you have a choice of which to do.

8.1 META-LEVELS AND HIERARCHICAL PLANNERS

The standard way to get out of this 'which method should I pick?' problem is to have a separate scheduler to handle the conflict resolution rules. In AI terminology, the things you can manipulate with the actions are in the *object-level*; these actions, which change the objects from one state to another with respect to the application domain are at the *task-level*; the conflict resolution rules which decide which task domain actions ought to be performed next are at the *planning-level*, and the operators that determine which planning actions to do next make up the *meta-level*. Meta, in this context, means 'above', and meta-rules are rules which do things to the level below, in this case the planning level.

So why stop at the meta-level? What if there are several meta-operators which you could apply to pick which planning strategy to use to decide which action to perform next so as to change the world to the next state? Well in theory there is nothing to stop you having a meta-meta-level, or any more above that. In practice, you rarely need to go above the straightforward meta-level.

You may also want to 'cross' levels. Suppose you had a plan which mixed planning and ordinary actions, like this: 'I'll walk to my new car, ask a few people if they know how to start it, then decide which route to take to Scotland, and finally drive there'. Here, items such as 'car' and 'Scotland' are at the object level; walking to the car and driving to Scotland are ordinary task-level actions (which you can just 'do' without thinking). Deciding which route to take to get there is a planning action, while asking a few people how to start the car is a meta-level action (you have to decide which of their proposed plans to use). Most conventional planners can't handle such cross level plans, but if the levels are removed (by making 'plan' an object in the world), then they can be handled with ease.

Apart from the object/action/planner/meta-planner hierarchy, there is another kind of hierarchy in plans. This is the *expands to* hierarchy, and it plays roughly the same role as subroutine calls do in programming languages. To distinguish between the two kinds, planners which make use of the first kind of planning are known as *meta-planners*, while the second kind are called *hierarchical planners*. The hierarchy is often described as consisting of various 'levels of abstraction'. The idea is that if someone wants to do something, they are unlikely to want to know *all* the details. If I asked 'how do I get to London?', I would be justifiably annoyed to receive and answer which began 'straighten the muscles at the back of your right leg such that they cause it to bend to a 45 degree angle, as your weight transfers to your left leg, loosen the muscles such that they extend your right leg out a metre in front of you . . .'. It's far too detailed when all I really wanted was 'take the A12', or 'catch a train'.

With a hierarchy, the solution is only given at the top level. If you don't understand some of the component actions, they can be expanded into simpler ones. Thus, by repeatedly asking 'how do I do that?' to the solution of how to get to London, you might get successively more detailed answers starting with 'catch the train', then 'catch the bus to the train station', 'walk to the bus stop', 'leave the room', 'open the door', 'turn the handle', 'perform an anticlockwise rotation of sufficient torque to cause the handle to turn', and so on.

There is yet a third way to plan, which gives us *non-linear planners*. Here, you account for things which can be done at the same time. This is especially useful if you're planning a task involving a number of people such as building a bridge. It is also useful in cases where several actions have to be performed concurrently (cut the meat while you're chewing the potatoes). Non-linear planning is currently the trendiest thing to put in your system, because it has a lot of practical applications. It looks very much like the kind of things people in Operational Research do, and there is a lot of overlap between these two approaches.

All of these methods of planning can be incorporated into the same planner, by the way, they're not mutually exclusive.

8.2 REPRESENTING PLANS

Plans are made up of actions, and actions are things which, when executed, change the world. In most planning systems, the world is represented by a collection of Frames, or Predicate Calculus assertions. This is very like the way it is used in a MUD. The way actions are represented, not surprisingly, is also in terms of Frames. Most actions will be made up of others, for example 'to have a meal' is made up of 'travel to the restaurant', 'order the meal', 'eat the meal', 'pay the bill' and 'travel back home'. 'Order the meal' would be made up of 'summon the waiter', 'obtain the menu', 'read the menu' and 'select the dish'. This kind of expansion can go on for as long as you like, but it has to finish somewhere. There has to be an ultimate set of 'primitive' actions which you can't expand, only execute. Exactly where these are pitched, you'll recall, can have a strong influence on the Frame Problem.

These primitive actions can, themselves, be represented in a number of ways. In planning terms, they usually have a *schema* containing information which defines the effects the action has on the world. Since all actions change the world in some manner, the normal way to do things is to list all the assertions which are true in the new state and which aren't necessarily true in the old one (prior to the execution of the action). Similarly, you can list all the ones which are no longer true in the new state but which were true before. The former is called the *add-list*, the latter the *delete-list*. If a fact is in neither the add-list nor the delete-list, you can assume that you should leave it unchanged (this is called the *STRIPS assumption*, named after the early planner which first used it).

So for an action like `[move,object,location]`, which would be used by a robot hand in building a pile of toy bricks, the delete-list would contain information saying that the object is no longer to be considered as being in the location it was in before, and neither is the hand; the add-list says that both are in the new location. There may be a need for additional tests to determine whether other objects fall over or are otherwise affected by the move – but cascade effects like this can quickly lead you back to the Frame Problem (which is, finding where to stop).

Primitive actions also have a third list, the *precondition-list*. This is quite often identical to the delete-list, and it lists the facts which have to be true in the world for the action to be performed. So you couldn't `[move,object,location]` unless the hand were holding the object – the `holding` slot for the hand must contain a pointer to the `object`'s Frame.

We can now see how forward-running and backward-running processes work. When forward-running you look at the current world state and pick out all the actions whose preconditions apply. You choose one of these, and generate a new state from its add-list and delete-list. If no actions can be applied, you backtrack to the previous state and choose a different action from those with preconditions which matched. You stop when you get to a state which satisfies the goal constraints.

When backward-running, look at the goal state and see what actions could have been executed to get you there. Pick one of these and test whether its preconditions are true in the initial state. If they are, then you've finished, otherwise you need to see what actions you would have to apply to get these preconditions to be true. If there are none, then you have to backtrack again.

Both of these ways of planning (as described) assume depth-first searches; breadth-first is probably better if you have no meta-rules to do the choosing for you, although it's not so easy to explain.

This representation of primitive actions in terms of an add-list, a delete-list and a precondition-list, fits very well into the way actions are represented in MUDs. You can make a case Frame for a primitive action which contains three slots, one for each list. When the primitive action is executed, the preconditions are checked and, if they pass, then the add-list is added to, and the delete-list is deleted from, the database. In order to make this work for input/output primitives, you will arrange things so that adding a fact to a player's `senses` slot will be spotted by the interpreter and will cause a message to be printed out on their screen. Add-list and delete-list representations are very easy to implement, and for this reason alone they should be considered by anyone planning on writing a flexible yet portable adventure.

8.3 INTELLIGENT MOBILES

There is another reason why add-lists and delete-lists are good news as far as representing actions in a MUD is concerned, and that is that the planning algorithms already exist for them. Why would you want to plan in a MUD, though? The actions are only meant for the players, aren't they? So why would the rest of the game have any cause to plan? Well, although actions are created mainly for the players, players aren't the only things in the game which might want to use them.

Mobiles, as I mentioned earlier, are objects which can move around the game. They can also execute commands, just like players. The normal way to go about this is to program them in advance, ie. just run down a little check-list every time a mobile enters a room to determine whether there is anything to do: 'oh, a player, I'll attack them'. However, you will then have to work out what the mobiles should do under all possible situations. Furthermore, since this will make your mobiles fairly predictable, the players will soon get to know what a mobile is going do under any given circumstance (unless they're just random).

What if the mobiles could do a bit more 'thinking' for themselves? If you could just tell them that to go out and get as much treasure as possible, then wouldn't it be great if that was *all* you had to tell them? Then they'd go off and figure out for themselves how to get the treasure. You can *do* this, with planning systems! If you make all mobiles planners, and give them a goal, then they could trundle around the database executing commands and trying to satisfy their goals, entirely off their own bat, while you sit and watch.

Even relatively primitive planners are able to do this quite well. With an ordinary backward-running search strategy, the robot could 'reason' through things like 'I need the gold but if I were to get it the troll would crush me. In order to stop the troll crushing me I need to kill it, and in order to do that I need a weapon. If I instantiate this weapon to be the axe, then I need to get the axe, and to do that I need to be where the axe is. The axe is in the hut, so I must be in the hut. In order to achieve that, I need to be in a room next to the hut, then I can move in. Ah, I am in a room next to the hut, so I'll move there then I can get the axe. Then I will have to move back here because in moving to the hut I made it so I was no longer in the same room as the troll, and I need to be if I'm to kill it with the axe.'.

The mobile may be surprised if it got to the hut and there was no axe (due, perhaps, to some other player or mobile taking it first), and it would have to re-plan. Re-planning during the execution of a plan is quite complicated, as you have to try to retain as much of the original plan as possible. This is necessary as the environment is 'dynamic' – it can change as a result of actions out of the control of the planner.

If all the players were mobiles, what results is a 'multi-actor' system. The official term for a planner which exists in an environment shared by other planners is an *actor* or *agent*. This kind of system is also very complicated because actors need to be able to co-operate in some ways, and even to counter-plan if their goals conflict. Putting humans in along with them is virtually unheard of, and yet this is exactly what AI researchers have been hoping to be able to do for years. With MUDS, they can!

Unfortunately, the large and powerful planning systems needed to do all this need large, powerful computers to run on. An ordinary interpreter would be very unlikely to be able to cope with them. So probably, for a MUD, the mobiles would run on a separate machine, linked to the game in the same manner as the real-life players. That way, they wouldn't even be able to cheat by looking directly at memory to find out whether the other players in the game were humans or other mobiles! Humans could still manage this, though, since planners aren't yet good enough to make passing the Turing Test a possibility within the near future.

8.4 EXPERT SYSTEMS

Expert systems (ESs) and planners are certainly very closely related, although whether planners are a kind of expert system, or expert systems are a kind of planner isn't really agreed! Expert systems definitely perform the same functions as planners, but in very different ways, and in highly specialised domains.

The rationale behind expert systems is that, for certain tasks in very complicated applications, there is always a large amount of domain-dependent knowledge involved. This means that you can't use any general methods to find out information and you will need to resort to methods specialised for the domain. The way the knowledge is organised is also dependent upon the domain, whether that domain is diagnosing rare blood diseases, looking for oil wells in Texas, or analysing the chemical structure of complex molecules from their nuclear magnetic resonance traces.

The procedure of building up a knowledge base for a specific domain is known as *knowledge acquisition*. Starting with a human expert such as a doctor, an engineer, a chemist or whatever, you ask a wide range of questions to try and find out just what it is they know about their subject. You code this up, usually as a set of rules, and often with some kind of numeric weighting attached to estimate the likelihood of a rule being applicable ('sometimes you find oil near the surface in this rock formation type, but not often').

Expert systems are the leading edge in practical AI research, particularly since they are supposed to be actually *useful*. Many are: for example, you can find expert systems for answering tax queries or for detailing your social security benefits and even for telling horoscopes. However, systems such as these are only superficially impressive, and are often not very complicated.

The problem is that expert systems use numeric – rather than symbolic – data to decide which of several alternatives to choose. The weightings attached to each piece of knowledge are combined in some way to determine which is the best choice at a particular place. This process of obtaining new facts, with a plausibility rating based on the old facts used in their deduction, is called *inference*, and it's what distinguishes an ES from a straightforward 'applications program'.

However, with more than about three hundred or so rules most expert systems break down. The knowledge interacts so much that the searching strategy can't focus properly on the important questions it ought to be asking. Humans using the system would either find it flitting from subject to subject like a butterfly, or becoming obsessed with an apparently irrelevant line of questioning.

Also, there are few ESs which *really* work. The examples given above (finding oil and so on) are just about the only large-scale ones you hear about. Newer ESs stick to smaller domains, where they can achieve better results, particularly on low power computers.

A lot of work in the ES area at present is on *shells*. These are *inference engines*, supposedly able to take any suitably formatted knowledge base and produce an ES for that domain. They have not, in general, been successful, and this is partly due to the fact that ESs are meant to be very specialised programs. If you can extract a lot of general information from a domain, you normally don't need an expert anyway! Shells do provide a wide variety of tools for 'knowledge engineers' and they are well worth using to work out the most suitable inferencing mechanism for your application before you start writing your own version.

Part of the current interest in ESs is due to their early commercial successes in those limited areas where they are being applied effectively. Large amounts of money have been invested in the hope of attracting research in the area. This has worked, and many new ES projects have been set up, a large number of people now getting into expert systems from outside of AI. It's almost as if you could get a degree in one subject (accountancy, art or biology), use this background to write a program encapsulating some part of your subject, call it an 'expert system' and then qualify for a PhD! A little cynical, perhaps, but it is fair to say that many long-standing AI researchers feel that the money could be better spent if spread out a little to the people who were interested in AI in the first place.

In case you're wondering, there are actually some expert systems around which play games. There is a semi-random adventure game called ROGUE, which consists of a complex of rooms containing either treasure (magic, weapons, gold) or hazards (traps and monsters). The idea is to get as much treasure as you can before being killed by the bad guys. There are no other players around to mess you about, and the opposition doesn't have any measure of guile built in, so players can get quite good at the game. Regular players tend to follow the same pattern of actions because they keep encountering the same stylised situations, and once they've become used to play they can do it almost instinctively. A program has been written, ROG-O-MATIC, which does the same thing. It just plays ROGUE using the same input/output as the human players, and has every known strategy for playing ROGUE coded into it! It is very good, too, and holds the record for the maximum number of points scored in a single game. It is hopeless at any other game, and would be just as bad at ROGUE if the database were changed even slightly, but then expert systems are supposed to be highly specialised, anyway . . . .

Expert systems to play MUD might be able to cope with more mundane tasks, but they would never be able to take part in the game on a level comparable to the players. This is because the domain is always changing – there are always new players coming along, which the ES doesn't know about and won't be able to handle. In addition, the environment itself is too dynamic so that, although an ES might cope with a single-player adventure, the same claim could be made for a program consisting solely of output statements that printed on the screen a set list of commands which got it to the end every time. There is indeed a lot of knowledge in an adventure, especially a MUD, but there is also a great deal of additional material which can change without warning. And if there is one thing expert systems positively cannot handle, it is learning arbitrary new facts.

8.5 MACHINE LEARNING

Learning is the single most difficult subfield of AI. Research has barely scratched the surface of what needs to be done – even though learning is a concept central to any definition of intelligence. If you can't learn things and so change your beliefs about the world, then you can't really be considered intelligent.

I won't go into the subject too deeply here, I'll just point out where learning can rear its ugly head in adventure games. The obvious place to look first is the mobiles. If these are going to be able to react to new situations and to new players, they must have some way of learning, some way of updating their knowledge structures to account for new information. Even if the knowledge already exists in a readable form, as it would if, say, the mobile was in conversation with another mobile and could access its memory directly, the new knowledge still needs to be assimilated with respect to the knowledge the mobile already has. Direct transference of sub-Frames does not work, because the Frames the mobile already possesses in its memory will be so interwoven that meshing them with a similar structure from another mobile would be next to impossible, except incrementally, ie. adding a small piece at a time).

Learning things from humans is even harder. Traditionally, Machine Learning comes at several different levels, including learning by being programmed, by being taught, by observation, by discovery, and by accident! Each of these assumes an entity which is to learn, and another entity posessing the knowledge which the learner must obtain. The learning process can be biased in favour of one or the other (the teacher does all the work when the pupil learns by being programmed, whereas the teacher does nothing at all if the pupil learns by discovery or experimentation – in effect, the environment itself acts as teacher).

For a mobile, then, it must ideally be able to perform at all levels. Obviously a mobile can be programmed, and it can be 'instructed', too, to some extent. This latter approach needs a modest natural language ability which can tie new words to the Frames held in its knowledge base in a manner suggested by the input. It's not too easy, but it can be done. Problems appear, though, in that you can easily design a mobile which believes absolutely everything you tell it – until it finds a contradiction. It must then decide which fact is right, and throw one away. However, to do this it must have some kind of 'plausibility' test for new information; this would involve assessing the likelihood that the new fact is actually true (or not). Once you get into this area of comparing the relative merits of information coming from various sources, you find yourself treading on some very dodgy ground indeed.

Learning by observation is another notion which looks easy, but isn't. Watching what people or other mobiles are doing, and trying to figure out their plans (so that you can either counter them or use them yourself) is called *plan recognition*. It is a slow and steady process, and, as with other aspects of learning, once you dip your foot into the mire you begin to wonder how on earth human beings manage at all! Every action observed will need to be tagged with an 'intention', related to the goals of the actor being watched. When some end result is observed, then the plans can be generalised and used.

There are plenty of other problems in goal recognition. For example, imagine you're watching an actor, Rupert. He goes to a refrigerator, removes some eggs, milk and butter goes over to a cupboard and gets out some flour and sugar, then sticks the lot in a bowl and proceeds to beat the mixture vigorously. After that, he puts it in an oven, walks away, comes back some time later and removes what looks like a cake. He plonks it on a plate, waits a while, then eats it all with a large spoon. Finally he washes the plate up and puts it away. A human being watching all this would guess that Rupert was hungry and wanted to eat a cake, so he made one – and that was that. A plan recogniser which possessed knowledge about what you have to do to make cakes would also reach the same conclusion. A plan recogniser which had never seen a cake before might deduce that Rupert wanted to wash his plate, and went through this long process in order to dirty it, so he could stick it under a tap and finally satisfy his goal!

8.6 BELIEF SYSTEMS

Another big problem in learning, and an area where it interacts with natural language a lot, is belief systems. These are ways in which the actor models what it thinks another actor thinks. If I believe that the moon is made of green cheese, then you may believe I believe it; in turn, I may believe you believe that, and you may believe I believe you believe I believe the moon is made of green cheese. Of course we could go on indefinitely in this manner, and eventually reach a state which is called *mutual belief*. After a certain point, you simply make the jump all the way – 'Right, so we both know as many beliefs as we want to about it'. It can get more confusing yet: for example I may believe that you believe I believe the moon is made of green cheese, but in reality I know that I believe that it isn't; I believe *you* don't know that's what I believe, though!

Most of the time, humans 'escape' from the system at about level three. They can stay as deep as they like, though, and work has even been done to show that in certain spy novels, the antagonists can have a set of nested beliefs to four or more levels deep. The depth is finite, however, not infinite, which is where the problems start to occur in any analysis of the situation.

Belief systems come up in Natural Language in the area of communication actions. If I wish to say something to you, then I need to have some model of you in order to gauge what I should say. Running up and panting 'Paddington?' at you would probably elicit nothing more than a suspicious look, but if I did the same thing to a ticket collector at a train station, they'd know what I meant. That's because I have a set of beliefs about ticket collectors, and they have a compatible set about travellers.

Similarly, if I were in a room and said 'it's cold in here' after you'd just walked in, the message I might actually wish to convey could be 'close the door you oaf!'. I probably used the former phrase in order to obtain a more favourable response, because I used my model of your beliefs about the world (and about myself) to predict the most likely reactions to the alternate ways of putting it – and chose the one where I didn't get my arm broken. Treating communication actions just like other actions, which can be fitted into plans and which can be planned for themselves, is known as the theory of *speech acts* in AI.

Representing recursive structures like belief systems is very difficult. Getting to the state where you can make the 'oh what's the point in going any further, we *both* know what the other knows!' inductive leap is even harder. If the actor tries to 'model' the user, then the user will adjust their own model of the actor, which will then have to re-adjust its model, and so on. At the moment, humans are more 'meta' than computers, and hence are invariably one step ahead of them. Eventually, perhaps, computers may be able to compete on more equal terms.

The problem of not being able to cope with mutual belief is well illustrated by the 'Japanese businessmen' example. The story is that two Japanese businessmen go to a conference in Tokyo, and strike up a very good friendship. They resolve to meet again, at a later, very important and prestigious conference in Osaka. One of them is unsure whether or not he can make it, however, and this is cause for some concern. Osaka conferences are governed by strict social rules, and if you don't turn up with a partner, then you are obliged to commit ritual suicide in front of the other delegates. Obviously, neither of the two businessmen wants *that* to happen to him! So the one with the possible date clash says he'll write to the other one if he finds it's OK, otherwise he won't.

When he gets back home, the businessman checks his diary and, sure enough, he is free on the date of the Osaka conference. So he writes a letter to his friend saying he can make it. Then a terrible thought occurs to him: the Japanese post office has a notorious reputation for losing letters, and what if this message to his friend never got through? Then his friend wouldn't come, and he'd have to commit hara-kiri! So he adds a line to the bottom (or is it the top for Japanese writing?) saying that he'd appreciate it if his friend wrote back saying the letter had made it to him, so he could be sure they would be both be going.

The second businessman duly finds the letter on his doormat, because the Japanese post office is in fact 100% efficient and doesn't deserve the bad name it has somehow picked up. He is pleased the meeting is on, and writes back confirming that he got the first businessman's letter. However, it strikes him that the post office could lose his own letter, and how would his friend then know that they were to meet? So he writes back asking for a letter saying that this one has arrived safely. His friend receives it, writes back thanking him for the letter, and asks for one to ensure that this message reached its destination. And so on, they both keep writing to each other saying they will go to the conference, but only if they get a letter confirming the fact that the other businessman received their own letter safely.

Now it's obvious that, without access to telephones, this could go on indefinitely. Both businessmen have every intention of going to the Osaka conference, but as long as they believe the Japanese post office is not perfect, they'll not go. One of them would have to say 'what the hell, we're going to go anyway, surely even if he *doesn't* get my letter he'll turn up?', and not bother writing any more. Of course, he'd always bear the nagging doubt that if his letter saying as much got lost in the post, he'd end up in a rather embarrassing situation!

This is quite similar to the way computer-run actors behave. Either they believe everything they're told, or they try to model the source of any information so they can gauge its trustworthiness. Even if this source is friendly, the nested models can become quite alarmingly difficult to follow. How humans manage to escape from the mess is not yet fully understood.

8.7 EPISODIC AND SEMANTIC MEMORY

If a mobile is unable to learn, it should at least give the impression that it can! A 'memory' is better than nothing. Hence, the best thing to do is to remember what has happened, and work on that. So if it comes across the same person as it has before, it can say 'Hello again, Pete!' instead of just a wary 'Hello . . . ?'.

This is called *episodic memory*, memory of actual events which have taken place. Episodic memory is not too hard to represent, and is best managed as a set of instantiated action schemas ('first he did a `[dig,hole]`, where `hole`=hole5, then a `[drop,box,hole]`, where `box`=box1 and `hole`=hole5'). This is just like a 'tape recording' of what has gone on, and in that sense would be better over a long period of time than most humans could manage.

The hard part is trying to update the action schemata themselves. These lie in what is called *semantic memory*, as they don't refer to actual events which have taken place, but to generalised events, which are abstract descriptions of what would happen if you were to execute them under certain conditions. The Case Frames used in the deep parse are a good example. It is still a mystery, to AI people and psychologists alike, as to how humans can do this as easily as they appear to be able to. It seems that rote learning, the mindless repetition of information until it sinks in (like absorbing the 'times table' at school) is one way to do it, but humans often seem to manage to pick up generalised actions from only one example, and sometimes from none at all (in cases where they 'invent it' themselves).

A certain amount of generalisation can be used in a hierarchically-based system, such as the Frames hierarchy I have already described. Here, when a sequence of actions is observed, the objects used are taken as far up the instantiation tree as they will go without violating any actions' preconditions which require them to be of a certain type. This is done for every action in the observed sequence, and what results is either a known elaboration of an already existing action which solves the task, or a new way to do it. If the former, then the goals can be hypothesised; if the latter, the goals must be supplied and then a new action can be created which uses the generalised version of those steps which were observed as its expansion.

There are obvious problems with this. The sequence of actions will most probably be linear, but order may in fact be irrelevant ('aha, so you have to put your *right* sock on first!'). Also, there may be spurious actions, arising from interleaved plans ('hmm, he picked up the bag, put his hand in it, sneezed, and pulled out a small furry mammal'). So it's not as simple as it seems. It's still better than nothing, though, if kept under proper control so that memory is not filled up with one-off irrelevancies. One approach is to keep a check how many times a sequence of actions is executed over a period of time, before admitting it to the semantic memory.

In a highly constrained environment, especially one where the actor is the only agent capable of changing its behaviour, such a system can actually perform quite well. Indeed, for some types of environment it may become *too* expert, and out-perform humans. This will especially be the case if the world is 'meaningless' to humans, consisting of strange objects with an inscrutable pattern of behaviour, reacting according to some internally-defined function based on time, presence of other objects, or whatever. Humans generally can't be bothered with such complex, yet uninteresting environments. Make the objects be wild animals in the jungle, or fantasy creatures in a dungeon, and if the function which controls their behaviour is actually a reasonable model of what they *ought* to do in that context, then people will enjoy the experiment ('game' to them) and might once again be able to out-perform the computer.

I've talked here about learning from the point of view of the mobiles. In fact, there is another way it can be applied: 'user modelling'. With this, the computer keeps a record of how players behave, and how they gradually gain experience in the game. Then, if they get stuck and ask for help, advice can be offered which ties in to what they already know. It is, for example, easier to explain what was wrong with an operating system command to 'print on the printer' if the user knows what a file is.

The most successful Machine Learning program to date is EURISKO (mentioned early in this book) which manages very ably to change its own control structure so that it improves with time. However, a lot of its power derives from what the author calls 'synergy', but which you or I would call 'tweaking'. That means some human being takes a look, from time to time, at the rules the program has developed and purges the most useless of them. Also, EURISKO only works well in an environment which it has totally under its own, absolute control. How it would fare in a MUD, against a dynamic environment, has not really been explored (but it looks rather less attractive a proposition than the stand-alone case).

User modelling is becoming increasingly popular, but isn't really necessary in adventure games. Part of the fun is, after all, in discovering the commands anyway. Simple commands are still understood, it's only in diagnosing incorrect input that a user model would come in handy. As with all systems of this kind, however, although the computer may be pretty smart in modelling the user, the user is almost certainly going to be modelling the computer too! Hence, when the machine thinks the user has given a confused command and is in need of an explanation, there is always the possibility that the user has given it because they *want* an explanation! Eliciting free information from the game in this way could become quite a skill in itself!

8.8 CONCLUSION

The central theme running through all the chapters is that Artificial Intelligence and computer games, particularly adventures, go very well with each other. I have sought to bring the two together at a sufficient level of complexity to show that both parties can benefit.

If you are a computer games person, it should be clear to you now that AI has more to offer than just Game Theory for chess and draughts programs. You should also have picked up a basic grounding in the subject en route and, with a bit of effort, could probably implement at least part of an adventure game based on the AI techniques I have outlined. If you now want to go further into the subject, there are plenty of readable books which pick on particular aspects of AI and explore or describe work in that area. Some of these are listed in the bibliography at the end.

Less can be said if you are already versed in AI, because unfortunately there are relatively few books about writing adventure games. Those that do exist invariably start off saying that the most important part of an adventure game is its 'plot' (which it is, but only if you're a player), and then discuss at great length how to write an adventure in a particular language (which will be either BASIC or machine code), and often tied very firmly to a particular make of home computer. Any AI relevance which these books do purport to possess is usually negligible, and very low-level. You will, however, find useful sections on how to design your adventure scenario, which may be of help to people who aren't brought up on science fiction or fantasy role-playing games; the implementation stage can generally be safely ignored. There are some very good, useful papers on ZORK around, however, and these are included in the bibliography. A look at some of the adventure-designing programs, such as THE QUILL, might be valuable if you are interested in the area and have a suitable computer to run it.

So what does the future hold for both AI and computer games? AI is still very much on the up-and-up, although it will probably go through a difficult patch in the not-so-distant future, when Alvey, ESPRIT, and the fifth generation programmes come to an end. This will especially be the case if they do not appear as successful as had been hoped. Many research groups are starting to look to AI as a way of getting extra funds, and they often do not have a complete, in-depth grasp of the subject before they do so. In particular, the expert systems community seems to include a lot of people with very plain ideas on what they want to do, and how it should be done, but only in their particular application domain. The people who have been involved with expert systems from the start are both excited and appalled at all this. Excited, because with all the extra effort involved, there is a good chance of significant advances in the field. Appalled because so many people are taking to the area with little or no background in AI that they are unlikely to produce any valuable results, and the whole field could be discredited.

Computer games are reaching a plateau now in their development. The limits of present-day machines have been reached, and with more powerful computers becoming available all the time, new games will be required. The fancier the graphics, the wider the choice of sound-effects, and the greater the complexity of the game, then the harder it will be for individuals to write arcade style programs on their own. Already the arcade market is running out of subjects for games, and is turning to 'big name' products such as DALEY THOMPSON'S DECATHLON and GHOSTBUSTERS. Even adventure games aren't beyond this sort of thing, for example Infocom's THE HITCH-HIKER'S GUIDE TO THE GALAXY game, and of course Adventure International ('AI'!) with their comic-book superhero series.

It would appear, then, that both AI and computer games are in for a rough ride over the next few years. It would be wildly optimistic to suggest that combining work from the areas would make one iota of difference to this, indeed the AI side is likely to remain especially impervious to any suggestion that they sully their hands with mere games (although MUDs don't *have* to be games of course, they are also very useful in educational and business domains and a lot more besides!). However, if a commercial MUD were a success, then the computer games companies would certainly sit up and take notice of AI, and with possibly spectacular results.

There are other reasons for running multi-user games, too. Software piracy, for example, is causing a huge drain on resources. There are, at the moment, no legal ways to stop someone abroad copying software and distributing it as their own in that country. No matter how sophisticated the mechanisms for thwarting copying, the only one which is guaranteed to succeed is not letting anyone get their hands on the software in the first place!

Actually this isn't as stupid as it sounds. With MUDs, the game can be run on a remote system, and the players' computers merely act as dumb terminals to the game. They transmit data to and from the program, but never get a copy of its main code into their own memory. Hence, players can't steal it. The problems here are that the communication links may be slow and expensive, and that for games with more than a handful of players there aren't many low-cost computers that pack enough oomph to run such a set-up.

Adventure games and communications are two of the main aspects of home computing which are becoming of increasing interest to users, the rest having peaked already. Perhaps an amalgamation of the two, in the form of a MUD, would be a success? We shall soon find out. There are several companies working on MUDs at the time of writing, and presently the games will begin to appear. Already, amateur versions of multi-player adventures are starting to spring up all around, in the same manner as bulletin boards. Some of the big networks, including Prestel/Micronet in Britain and Compuserve in the USA, are known to be planning MUDs, too. With even more AI principles taken on board, these games could become vast, very complex, and thoroughly addictive. Above all, they'd be tremendous fun!

So there is a niche for AI in computer games, and there is a place for computer games in pure AI research. All that's needed is for someone to point out the fact, examine the places where the overlap would be greatest and most useful, and give a little insight into what would be involved in such a marriage. Hopefully, this book has gone some way to meeting that need.

APPENDIX 1

BIBLIOGRAPHY

INTRODUCTION

This Appendix is a collection of publications which readers may find relevant. Rather than list all the references I have on a particular subject, most of which would be useless if you have no background in the appropriate area, I have decided instead to give an annotated list of key books and research papers on the topics I have covered.

There are two kinds of work in this bibliography. The first is the general background kind, which contains all the information you need to get a grounding in the subject, together with pointers to more detailed, relevant, in-depth information (if there is any!). Many papers of this kind are the ones where the ideas were originally introduced in the first place. As such, they are quite old, and are no longer state-of-the-art. They do, however, tend to be non-technical, and hence may be a useful read for beginners who can get hold of them.

The second kind of work is the introductory text. These tend to be much more up-to-date, and contain references to a host of other publications (including many in the first list!). They are pitched at a level with which the intelligent novice may be able to cope.

Both these types are split into those suitable for people who know nothing about computer games, and those for people who know nothing about Artificial Intelligence. It is on this basis that I have organised the bibliography.

If you have difficulty in getting copies of any books, your local library should be able to help, using inter-library loan. The information I have included is enough to pin down any of the reference works mentioned. However, some of the more esoteric background works will probably be in a different league to the usual requests handled by a branch library, and if you do want to follow them up it may mean a trip to either your local university or the British Library.

INTRODUCTORY READING FOR AI NOVICES

These are works which anyone considering working seriously in AI ought to look at.

The Handbook of Artificial Intelligence
A. Barr & E. A. Feigenbaum
Pitman (London, 1981)

If you want to get into AI, you *must* buy this book. It is a bible for AI researchers. Every major AI idea is covered in it, and even specific program implementations are discussed in detail. It is a complete reference book, an encyclopedia for the subject. It has pointers to where further details may be found, but in general the brief descriptions it gives on topics of interest are so good that unless you want to study some particular aspect of AI in depth, you needn't bother looking up the references. It comes in three volumes, the first of which is the best (the other two are pretty expensive!). A very important work for the serious AI student. Saves you hours of time if you want to find out what something means!

Programming in PROLOG
W. F. Clocksin & C. S. Mellish
Springer-Verlag (Heidelberg, 1981)

This is a very solid, professional book which describes everything you ever wanted to know about the language PROLOG. It also has many practical examples, and these are of invaluable help to people learning AI techniques (if they have a PROLOG interpreter to hand). It is clear and well-structured, in fact I use it myself for teaching the language to students!

LISP
P.H. Winston & B.K.P. Horn
Addison-Wesley (Reading, Mass., 1981)

LISP is the most important AI language in use. This book is a fairly good introduction to it, and is full of exercises (and solutions!). There are some LISP implementations of AI ideas, for example Frames, ATNs and productions systems, and it's the standard introductory text at most LISP courses in universities. There are many other books on LISP, but this is about the best – especially if you want to know how to *use* it, not just find out what it looks like!

Principles of Artificial Intelligence
N.J. Nilsson
Springer-Verlag (Heidelberg, 1980)

The theoretical basis underlying AI. It starts from production systems (which I have mentioned only briefly in this book, but which are quite important), and works up through Predicate Calculus, to a system of entities called *units*, which are essentially just Frames. It then uses these to develop some planning systems. Very good, and although it talks about AI from a mainly theoretical standpoint, it never gets so bogged down in symbols that you don't know what's going on. You ought to get hold of this if you want to make an effort to learn more about AI.

BACKGROUND READING FOR AI NOVICES

These are the works you might want to read to uncover the heart of some aspect of AI.

The Theory and Practice of Augmented Transition Networks
M. Bates
From: Natural Language Communication with Computers, edited by L. Bolc (pp 191 – 259)
Springer-Verlag (New York, 1978)

You want to know about ATNs? Well this is the paper which spills the beans. Fluent, lucid, plenty of examples and diagrams, this is just how a paper *should* be written. Everything is set out clearly.

Experience with KRL-0
D.G. Bobrow & T. Winograd
From: International Joint Conference on Artificial Intelligence no. 5, 1977

This paper describes KRL-0 (KRL stands for Knowledge Representation Language). The KRL system was devised to test out the full power of Frames. Unfortunately, that meant it tried out *all* Frames' formidable number of associated features, and became so complex and confused that no-one had the faintest idea of what was going on. The structures it provided were *too* rich; there were any number of ways to represent the same fact, without any one of them being a more obvious choice than the others. The authors describe their bitter experiences, a warning to others against repeating their mistakes.

Case Systems for Natural Language
B. Bruce
From: Artificial Intelligence no. 6, 1975 (pp 327 – 360)
Netherlands, bi-monthly journal

A more up-to-date book about Case grammars. It assesses the work on Case grammars since Fillmore's first paper (see below), and it goes on to talk about future directions. A 'representative sample' of proposed case systems is taken, and examined in depth. For anyone interested in Natural Language, it's well worth a read; it's still quite good even if you're not interested!

PARRY Encounters the Doctor
V. Cerf
From: Datamation, July 1973 (pp 62 – 64)
USA, monthly magazine

The short paper which sets ELIZA against PARRY. Even for those without the slightest interest in either AI or computer games, this is worth a look at just for a bit of fun!

Syntactic Structures
N. Chomsky
Mouton (The Hague, 1957)

The one that gave Linguistics a shot in the arm. This book has had a profound influence on the subject, and indeed on many others. It introduces the various grammars (ie. types 0, 1, 2 and 3) found in languages, and makes the suggestion that there is more to language than just syntax. The book has been attacked and praised from all sides, but it remains one of the classic works in Linguistics (and hence in Natural Language). Not everyone's cup of tea, though, and it can get a bit obscure and heavy at times.

The Case for Case
C. J. Fillmore
From: Universals in Linguistic Theory
Edited by E. Bach & R. T. Harms (pp 1 – 88)
Holt, Rinehart & Winston (New York, 1968)

The first big paper on Case grammars, and one which has influenced Natural Language ever since. Worth reading if you can get hold of it, because it starts off assuming you know nothing about the subject (as at the time, no-one did). Things have gone a long way since then, and many different approaches have been proposed using the basic Case idea. A bit of a weighty read, full of diagrams.

The Frame Problem and Related Problems in Artificial Intelligence
P.J. Hayes
From: Artificial and Human Thinking
Edited by A. Elithorn & D. Jones (pp 45 – 49)
Jossey-Bass (San Francisco, 1973)

A shortish paper, which introduced the Frame problem to us all. It looks fairly difficult, due to a preponderance of mathematical symbols, but it's quite easy to follow, and certainly makes its point.

Try to read it if you want more detail on the theoretical side of the Frame problem (or didn't understand my own explanation!).

The Nature of Heuristics
D.B. Lenat
From: Artificial Intelligence no. 19, 1982 (pp 189 – 249)
Netherlands, bi-monthly journal

Lenat has written several papers on his program EURISKO, this is the main one. He talks at length about heuretics (the study of heuristics), and goes on at understandably great length to describe EURISKO. Because the program is so important, there are further articles in a later issue of the journal (no. 21), which show some *very* impressive examples. Complex, but everything is explained from basics.

ROG-O-MATIC: A Belligerent Expert System
M. Mauldin et al.
From: Department of Computer Science, Carnegie Mellon University
Reference: CMU-CS-83-144, 1983

Technical, from the expert system point of view. You don't need to know the ROGUE game to understand it as it gives an outline of the game. It's very strongly honed for ROGUE, unfortunately, but it shows just what can be done if you want to compare human performance with that of a machine. ROG-O-MATIC, incidentally, is about fifty percent bigger than ROGUE itself!

Machine Learning
R.S. Michalski, J.G. Carbonell & T.J. Mitchell
Tioga (Paolo Alto, Calif., 1983)

The seminal work on Machine Learning. Useful for the references alone – it lists some 572 papers on Machine Learning at the back, coded by the subfields to which they are relevant. The book itself is a large collection of papers, in sections devoted to particular kinds of Machine Learning. You're bound to find at least four of these of use to you whatever your interests in AI. No other work on Machine Learning comes close to this one in comprehensiveness. No other work on machine learning comes close to costing as much, either . . . .

A Framework for Representing Knowledge
M. Minsky
From: The Psychology of Computer Vision
Edited by P.H. Winston (pp 211 – 277)
McGraw-Hill (New York, 1975)

This is the paper that introduced Frames to the world. Minsky goes on a bit about inheritance, but really it's only the basic ideas you'll need to look at. When it appeared, the paper caused a great stir in the AI world, and much excitement. A lot of work resulted from it, and it pulled AI out of the doldrums which had begun to set in the mid-70s. Riveting stuff, if only for his attack on logic towards the end!

The Organisation of Expert Systems: a Tutorial
M. Stefik et al.
From: Artificial Intelligence no. 18, 1982 (pp 135 – 173)
Netherlands, bi-monthly journal

If you want to know about expert systems, this is the paper for you. It's a very good description of all the major expert systems which are currently in favour, and it goes through the techniques they commonly use. Problems which arise from unreliable or variable data are pointed out, and solution methods given. A similar treatment is given to other aspects of ES domains. It is very detailed, but won't go over your head. Well worth a read to find out everything which expert systems have – and haven't – to offer.

Computing Machines & Intelligence
A. M. Turing
From: Computers & Thought
Edited by E.A. Feigenbaum & J. Feldman (pp 11 – 35)
McGraw-Hill (New York, 1963)

This is the original paper on the Turing Test (it's a reprint, it first appeared in 1953, but that's harder to get a copy of). In fact, it's probably fair to say that it's the very first paper on the subject of Artificial Intelligence itself! In it, Turing outlines his 'imitation game', and notes some of the arguments against using it to test for intelligence. These he takes and systematically destroys. Every AI researcher worthy of the name should have a copy of this paper lying around somewhere in their office.

INTRODUCTORY READING FOR COMPUTER GAME NOVICES

These are the only really technical papers I've come across relating to adventure games.

How to Fit a Large Program into a Small Machine
M.S. Blank & S.W. Galley
From: Creative Computing, July, 1980 (pp 80 – 87)
USA, bi-monthly magazine

A description of how to implement an adventure on a micro. There are many problems in doing this, but mainly text compression and how the interpreter should work. ZORK is translated into *Z-code*, which runs on a virtual machine. This machine is simulated by the interpreter, one of which can, in theory, be written for any target machine. You ought to get this paper if you're thinking of working on a large-scale adventure using a small-memory micro, but if you intend to use a thumping great big main frame then it's not going to be of so much interest to you.

ZORK: A Computerised Fantasy Simulation Game
P.D. Lebling, M.S. Blank & T.A. Anderson
From: IEEE Computers volume 12 no. 4, 1979 (pp 51 – 59)
USA, monthly magazine

This is *the* paper to read if you want to know about adventure games. It goes into total detail about the ZORK system, and is absolutely essential if you want to look at this area in depth. It gives examples of play, outlines the control flow, and provides sample object/action definitions in the ZORK internal format. Although it does illustrate some of the bother you have with an object-centred language, it is a very good, sound paper. Rush out and get yours now!

ZORK and the Future of Computerised Fantasy Simulations
P. D. Lebling
From: Byte, December 1980 (pp 172 – 182)
USA, monthly magazine

Really just a shorter version of the previous one, but easier to get a copy of. It goes into some detail of ZORK in play, but doesn't mention data structures or anything like that. It's a functional description, rather than an implementational one. It covers a lot of the basic concepts you're likely to want in any half-decent adventure game, and in a clear and readable fashion.

BACKGROUND READING FOR COMPUTER GAME NOVICES

You might want to chase up a few of these to get a feel for adventure games. In addition to these, most issues of the (now sadly defunct) magazine *Micro Adventurer* would be of help, especially the later ones.

An Adventure in Small Computer Game Simulation
S. Adams
From: Creative Computing, August 1979 (pp 90 – 97)
USA, bi-monthly magazine

Scott Adams is now immensely rich, and runs the company *Adventure International*. In this early paper, he describes how to go about writing an adventure game. The approach is essentially Frame based, but is very ad hoc and uses a lot of numeric, rather than symbolic, data; it is therefore quite hard to follow what's going on. It's fairly technical, and is based around an adventure definition language, which makes it quite interesting. Doubtless he wouldn't publish anything similar nowadays, for fear of giving away trade secrets!

A Voice from the Dungeon
R.A. Bartle
From: Practical Computing, December 1983 (pp 126 – 130)
UK, monthly magazine

Yes, it's by me. This is a general introduction to MUD, describing what the game is, how you play it, what you can do in it, and so on. It's not technical, and is fairly anecdotal, but it does contain some usable information, lurking below the surface. There are, at the time of writing, over a dozen other articles about MUD of a page in length or more, but they all say roughly the same thing as this one (except for a large variation on the number of players they claim MUD will take – the actual number in the original version is 36).

COMPUTE!'s Guide to Adventure Games
G. McGath
COMPUTE! Books (Greensboro, North Carolina, 1984)

A very nice piece of work. It describes the concept of adventure games, goes through a few examples, says how to play this type of game in general, outlines how they work (at present), and describes how to write your own. This last part is almost technical, and would be quite useful if it had been extended a little. This is certainly a very good book if you're interested in adventures, or if you are complete beginner in the subject.

Glorious MUD
R. A. Bartle
From: Practical Computing, January 1985 (pp 92 – 93)
UK, monthly magazine

Me again. This is a more practical guide to getting a MUD up and running. Although the article stops rather abruptly, this was due to editorial intervention which pushed it down to a manageable two pages, the original article was half as long again. The article is the sort of thing you might want to read if you're thinking of implementing a MUD yourself, because it outlines a few of the problems you're going to come up against. It's especially interesting if you're thinking of doing it commercially.

Kings of the Castle Walls
D. Ellis
From: Practical Computing, March 1982 (pp 89 – 93)
UK, monthly magazine

A fairly good history of adventure games. It outlines some of the principles involved, and gives a few fairly far-sighted views on what the world holds for adventure games in the future. Quite an interesting read, although MUD was already two years old when it was published, so some of its predictions had already come true.

Fantasy Games
D. Lubar
From: Creative Computing, March and May 1981
(pp 32 – 34 & 20 – 24)
USA, bi-monthly magazine

Really just a series of reviews of adventure games on the market at the time. Many hobby magazines on the stands today, for example *Computer & Video Games*, regularly have a similar collection of reviews of the more modern games. This one is sufficiently old that the concepts the writer thought of then as new (and hence described in full) are quite standard nowadays. If you know nothing of adventure games, reading this will give you a grounding on some of the features which aren't really considered important any more in the reviews of today.

Putting Adventure in Adventure Games
R. Plamondon
From: Creative Computing, August 1981 (pp 70 – 76)
USA, bi-monthly magazine

Describes a few of the dos and don'ts that make or break adventure games. It itemises some of them, and gives examples showing where they crop up. Fairly low-level and obvious, you can read this kind of thing in most hobby magazines nowadays. If you're an absolute beginner, though, it does point out a couple of the mistakes which present-day articles would take for granted that you know. It ends with a rather useless list of role-playing magazines you can buy (or could then!).

APPENDIX 2

GLOSSARY

This appendix provides a glossary of general terms used in this book and in and around both AI and computer games.

Adventure game
A kind of computer game based on the representation and control by the computer of an (usually imaginary) environment. Players take on the role of an explorer of this environment, and interact with the computer-generated situations which arise as a consequence of the actions they carry out in the environment (or are carried out by other actors sharing the same world). The term 'Adventure Game' is conveniently shortened to just 'adventure'.

AI
An abbreviation for *Artificial Intelligence*.

Arcade game
A computer game of the kind commonly found in amusement arcades. The vast majority of home-computer games are also arcade

games. Characterised by fast action, nifty graphics, and reliance on co-ordination skills.

Artificial Intelligence
A field of computer science which is devoted to finding ways of making machines (usually computers) appear to possess intelligence. There are many subfields within the area, ranging from perceptual problems (computer vision, speech recognition) through learning issues to higher matters (such as generating and understanding English text, planning and problem-solving and expert systems), with a whole bundle of other ideas on the side. Often mis-used in the popular computer press to mean techniques which hail from Artificial Intelligence research.

A-kind-of
Full form of `ako`.

Actions
Commands which the user of an adventure game may issue to the system and which the interpreter will find meaningful.

Add-list
The list of facts which are made true after the execution of a particular action.

Adjective
A word which amplifies the description of a noun, such as: long, heavy, broken, mispronounced, invisible, aged, benign.

Adverb
A word which amplifies the description of a verb, such as: rapidly, craftily, jauntily, comfortably, imaginatively, squarely, agonisingly.

Ako
Short for *a kind of*. Used in preference to *subset-of*. For example, under the `ako` slot for 'Durham', you might find the value 'city'.

Application domain
The field in which the program works, usually a non-AI subject which is receiving AI treatment. An expert system, for example, might have as its application domain the diagnosis of eye diseases.

Argument
A parameter of a function is an argument to that function.

Atomic

Indivisible. If something is atomic, it cannot be expressed in terms of something else. Propositions in the Propositional Calculus are atomic, as are integers and strings. Variables and lists are not atomic.

Automated office

A demonstrator project for combining several aspects of AI methodology. It's an attempt to create an environment in which business people can operate more effectively than they do at present, with many of their more mundane tasks carried out under computer control.

Axiom

An initial fact supplied as true.

Backward-running

Starting with detailed productions (*qv*), trying to generate a general production. For sets of condition/action rules (production systems), matching against actions then trying its condition. Same as *bottom-up*.

Boolean

Pertaining to the values true/false, named after the first person to study them in depth, George Boole.

Bottom-up

Starting with the most detailed and trying to get to the most general. The same as *backward-running*.

Computable

Able to be performed, in theory, on a sufficiently large computer. Whether a powerful enough computer exists or not is irrelevant. Most useful functions are computable, but some are not. For example, it is impossible to write a computer program which, given any computer program in a preselected high-level language, and the data upon which it is to be run, would be able to decide whether the program will halt in a finite time or not (which, incidentally, is called the 'halting problem').

Conjunction

A word which can be used to join two sentences together, for example: therefore, although, however, because, so, and, then.

Container
An object in an aventure game which can hold a list of other objects. As well as obvious objects like bags and sacks, players and rooms also act as containers.

Contradiction
The same as a fallacy: a sentence in logic which is always false.

DCG
Definite Clause Grammar.

Database
A collection of pieces of information describing a domain. In an adventure game context, normally the text in the definition language which describes the environment.

Definition language
Adventure games commonly are written from scratch in a language such as BASIC. The better ones use their own specialised language which is designed for the sole purpose of writing adventure games. Such a language is a definition language.

Delete-list
The list of facts which are made false after the execution of a particular action.

Demon
A piece of program which only runs after a certain event has taken place. This is normally when a predefined amount of time has elapsed, but is occasionally when a specific change has been made to the database. If I lit the fuse of a bomb, a demon would explode it after the requisite time had passed.

Demonstrator projects
Computer programs designed to show off the power and ability of existing software (usually an integration of several strands of development), rather than purely original work.

Dictionary
Another word for a *lexicon*.

Domain
An area of study. All programs work on some applications but cannot handle others; those it works for are its domain. For very

general programs, the domain will be quite large, and several distinct sub-domains may be covered, although there is usually a subsequent loss of detail within each one. With the onset of expert systems, these days the notion of a domain often carries connotations of a great deal of specificity – it is treated as a shorthand for *application domain.*

Domain-specific

Pertaining to only one application, generally in a lot of detail. Domain-specific knowledge is highly specialised for the particular area of study. For example, facts about chess which are domain-specific will not be of much use in any application apart from chess.

Dump file

Sometimes used as an intermediary between the compilation and interpretation phases of running a program. Often necessary if the interpreter is a pseudo-machine, in which case the dump file may contain some pseudo-code.

Element-of

A more understandable name for 'is-a' (*qv*).

Environment

Normally, a program's internal representation of an imaginary world. Occasionally, the world itself.

FOL

Short for *First Order Logic.*

FOPC

First Order Predicate Calculus.

Frame problem

The difficulties which arise in deciding the amount of detail in which to consider a domain. You can never get as deep as things are in real life, and whenever you do consider more detail, the interaction between the various objects in the world increases dramatically.

Fallacy

A sentence in logic which is always false.

Fire

The action of a demon coming to life and carrying out its associated function.

First order
A logic is first order if it only quantifies over objects, not predicates or functions or connectives. That means that variables may only be bound to objects or data structures, not to anything else.

Forward-running
Starting with a general production, try to generate more and more detailed productions. For sets of condition/action rules (production systems), matching against a condition then expanding its action. Same as *top-down*.

Front-end
Near to the user. Generally, it is either a computer which handles input/output so as to free another machine for processing, but occasionally programs which perform mundane but time-consuming tasks for another program. Natural Language front-ends to databases, for example, might translate English-like requests into a form the database management system can understand.

Game Theory
Nowadays, that part of Artificial Intelligence which is devoted to the study of two-player games, such as chess, Othello and backgammon. Normally a combination of highly domain-dependent heuristic evaluation functions, and a powerful search technique.

GPSG
Generalised Phrase-Structure Grammar.

Get file
Also called *include files* in some languages, these are slices of program which are textually substituted into the main program wherever they are referenced. Often used to link together modular languages, but also act as macros for repetitive common pieces of text.

Hack
A noun describing one of two things. Originally, a program which did the job it was intended to do, but had to have its arm twisted by cunning calls to the operating system, or many add-ons to catch odd bugs (*qv* hairy). Nowadays, more commonly used to describe the event of someone having broken through some kind of computerised security.

Hacker
One who *hacks*.

Hacking

The process of getting to grips with a computer, usually at the operating system or machine code level. 'To hack' is the verb which describes this. Nowadays, often mis-used to mean breaking into a system and probably playing merry hell with it.

Hairy

A term used by computer hackers to mean a program which has had lots and lots of little bits added to it in convoluted and ad hoc ways, in order to get round little problems which weren't at first envisaged by the programmer.

Hardwired

Computing term to mean a program has been built into the hardware. Used metaphorically to describe software constructs which would be incredibly difficult to change except by rewriting the program. The original MUD, for example, had a hardwired assumption that it would be have no more than thirty-six players.

Heuristic

A rule of thumb which gives a short-cut to finding a solution to a problem. Not always 100% guaranteed correct, and usually very domain-specific. It helps to cut down the amount of searching required to find a solution.

Host

The computer upon which the main part of a multi-user system runs.

Imitation game

Turing's name for the Turing Test.

Implementation

The process by which an original specification or idea is transformed into a working computer program, ie. the writing of a program to produce the results defined in the specification.

Individual

An individual is an entity in the First Order Predicate Calculus which may be bound to a variable. An atomic symbol.

Inference rule

A way of building new sentences from existing facts in a logic, for example modus ponens (*qv*).

Interpreter
A program which runs other programs. For example, LISP is a language which is generally interpreted, so the interpreter is a program which reads in LISP and translates it into some internal form which it can execute. Compiled programs are not interpreted, rather they drop straight relocatable binary files which can be run by the hardware. See also under *pseudo-machine*.

Is-a
A slot in a Frame, used to say that the Frame is an element of another Frame. Used in preference to *element-of*. If a route from York to Edinburgh went through Durham, then under the Frame for 'Durham' the `is-a` might have the value 'York to Edinburgh Journey'.

Knowledge Representation
The field of Artificial Intelligence devoted to the design and construction of effective ways to represent information. Often the structures are surprisingly general, despite the very specialised kind of knowledge found in many applications.

KR
Short for *Knowledge Representation*.

Knowledge engineer
Someone who tries to design knowledge bases for AI programs, especially for expert systems.

Lexicon
A list of words and their meanings at the syntactic level, ie. what parts of speech they are able to be. A table which relates words to the classes or parts of speech which they may take. For example, 'whistle' would have entries for noun ('do I hear a whistle?') and verb ('whistle me that tune again').

Library
A collection of useful routines which are common to many programs. Some languages, for example BCPL, have all their input/output procedures in libraries, which makes transporting BCPL programs from one installation to another easier, as most of the compiler will be the same and only the libraries need rewriting.

Log file
A verbatim record of an adventure game, sometimes called the *script* of a game.

Logic
A mathematically rigorous way of describing things. From an initial set of facts (axioms) and rules, other facts can be generated. Attempting to use a logic to determine whether a fact is true or false (or unknown) is the act of carrying out a proof.

Macro
Something which is a shorthand for something else. If, every time you refer to the macro, you mean something else, then that something else is the macro's *expansion*. A macro 'dismiss' may have as its expansion 'please go away, I find your presence irritating', in which case every time the word 'dismiss' was mentioned, it would be replaced by its expansion. Macros sometimes have parameters, and can be recursive.

Meta-level
When something is at a meta-level with respect to something else, it may manipulate that object and any properties it may possess. So meta-level operators can reason about the names of operators on the level below, about function bodies, and so on.

Mobile
An object in an adventure game which the program can control, although which may be handled by a human being. Most players will not be controlling mobiles, but some will. Non-player characters are mobiles which cannot be controlled by humans.

Modus ponens
The inference rule which says that if `P=>Q` is true and P is true then Q is true.

Multi-user
Able to handle several users simultaneously.

NPC
Short for *Non-Player Character*.

Non-directive
A psychological term which means that the person interviewing the

patient takes as little an active part in the conversation as possible, so that the patient can direct the conversation in any way they please.

Non-Player Character
A computer-controlled object in an adventure game. The object may move around and do many other things which a normal player might attempt. See also *mobile*.

Normalisation
The process of putting text into a standard format, for example converting it all to upper case, with tabs, multiple spaces and carriage returns converted to single spaces.

Noun
A 'name' word, such as: book, cord, pipe, hunger, idea, starling, electron.

Origins
A huge board games convention held in America. It covers all aspects of board games, including role-playing games such as DUNGEONS AND DRAGONS, RUNEQUEST and TRAVELLER.

Object
An entity in an adventure game. Most often it means some manipulatable item, such as a door or a kettle, but really includes things like players and rooms, too.

Off-line
Done by hand, or done at a leisurely place at some previous time by a computer.

Operator
A function which relates two states together. Usually it's an action, and executing the action takes you from one state to a new one which incorporates the effects of the action.

PSG
Phrase-Structure Grammar.

Persona
The role which a player of an adventure game takes on, when many such roles are possible. The name of the object as which the user wishes to play the game. If I commonly played as Kieran, Marmaduke and Lucretia, then these would all be my personas.

Player

Either the person playing in an adventure game, or the internal object in the game which the human being is controlling.

Plot

The logic behind the universe in an adventure game. Strong plots normally lead to quest-based games, ones which merely define the *raison d'etre* of the milieu tend to support points-based games.

Points

The scoring mechanism in many adventure games. Players accumulate points for their deeds and the treasures they retrieve, until some maximum is reached, or a threshhold passed.

Precondition-list

The list of facts which must all be true before a particular action may be executed.

Preconditions

Boolean functions which all need to come up true if a command is to be executed. For example, it is a precondition of writing a letter that you have a piece of paper. It's another that you have a pen or pencil. It is not a precondition that you must wear a hat.

Predicate

A boolean function. One which returns an answer of true or false.

Production system

A set of rules with a condition part (if) and an action part (then). These rules are sometimes called *productions*, other times *rewrite rules*. They can be run forwards or backwards. Either the conditions or actions are matched against a database, and if present then the other half of the rule is asserted into that database. A grammar specified in BNF can be used as a production system in parsing.

Property

Something which is true about an object. For example, an object might have a colour of red, a weight of 250 grams, and a shape of round, and these would all therefore be properties of that object. Sometimes a distinction is made between variable properties such as position, temperature and contents and more static ones like name, components and value.

Proposition
A statement in a logic which the person using the logic has declared is true.

Pseudo-code
The theoretical machine code for a pseudo-machine. Usually quite high-level.

Pseudo-machine
An imaginary machine which is designed to run a programming language interpreter. The machine could – theoretically – be built out of hardware, but is generally simulated in software. Programs written to run on the interpreter are translated directly into a set of pseudo-machine instructions. This approach is successful because it enables programs to be transported from one machine to another if an interpreter for the pseudo-machine instructions exists on the target machine.

Puppet
If, when playing an adventure game, you are required to give instructions which move around some internal player which just obeys your commands, then you are controlling a puppet. In normal adventures you move around some entity which represents you. Puppet games can generally be recognised by reporting events in the first person ('I see a snake here') rather than the second ('You see a beggar here').

Quest
The objective of certain adventure games. Rather than accumulate points, players have a goal which they have to achieve in order to win.

Room
An object in an adventure game which represents a location. Rooms link to other rooms for travel purposes, and are associated with a list of objects that represents their contents.

Satisfy
If X is an argument of a predicate P which is true, then X is said to *satisfy* P.

Second order
A second order logic allows quantification over predicates and functions as well as objects.

Sentence
In logic terms, a collection of propositions strung together with sentential connectives.

Sentential connective
Something which joins two propositions together in the Propositional Calculus. Examples include $\wedge$, $\vee$ and =>.

Specification
A description of the program, or other end product, which is required as the result of a proposed piece of work, usually provided either formally (eg. written down in some specification language) or informally (eg. verbally). Very general specifications which leave a lot up to the programmer are said to be 'loose', ones which describe the desired product in some detail are known as 'tight' or 'strict'.

State
A state is a representation of the world at a particular moment in time.

State-to-state diagram
A directed graph of states (nodes in the diagram) connected by arcs. One node is designated the start. Arcs leading from the current node are compared to the next element on some input string, and if one matches then the new current node is the one at the end of the arc.

Syntactically sugared
A device whereby a logic or language is made more expressive but no more powerful, by inventing constructs which are shorthand for more lengthy ones. The rules which translate from the ordinary syntax into the sugared version and back can be automated.

TG
Transformational Grammar.

Turing Test
The accepted way to determine whether or not a computer is intelligent, devised by Alan Turing. If, by asking questions of a computer and a human being, it is impossible to gauge on the basis of their responses alone which is which, the test is passed.

Tautology
A sentence in logic which is always true.

Tokenisation

The process of converting an ASCII string into an internal form, usually an integer unique to this word. This then becomes the *token* or *symbol* representing that word.

Top-down

Starting with the most general and trying to get to the most detailed. The same as *forward-running*.

Treasure

Objects in adventure games which can be translated into points in some way, usually by depositing them in some preset place.

Truth table

A mechanism whereby for all combinations of input and output in a boolean system, the truth value of the result is given. The truth table for '$\wedge$' is:

$true \wedge true \equiv true$
$true \wedge false \equiv false$
$false \wedge true \equiv false$
$false \wedge false \equiv false$

Universal specialisation

The inference rule which says that if we have an expression which is true for all values of X, and we have another expression which is the same as the first except that it's only for one individual, then we can deduce that this second expression is true.

Upward compatible

A system is upward compatible if it will work in a more complex system in its entirety, without any changes. Normally applied to bottom-of-the-range hardware which can be upgraded to better hardware without all the programs which run on the old equipment having to be rewritten. Programs which run on the new machines don't necessarily run on the old, however.

User

Someone who runs an interactive program. In an adventure game, a user would be a player.

Variable

A symbol in a logic which does not have a value, ie. is not bound to anything. Like a variable in a programming language. Usually a formal parameter of a function.

Verb

An 'action' word, such as: walk, talk, invite, own, think, estimate and inhibit.

Virtual machine

The same as a *pseudo-machine*.

Vocabulary

The words which an adventure game can accept, together with their associated meanings. Not the syntax, but occasionally it can include elements from the deep parse level of action definitions.

Walk

The way AI people describe the action of traversing a data structure, especially a list. Normally, the list is taken in order, the element currently under consideration being termed the *head*, and the unprocessed part of the list the *tail*.

World model

A program's internal representation of (normally) the real world. In 'planning' terms, the representation held by the actor of the environment in which it exists (which may or may not actually exist).

APPENDIX 3
ACRONYMS USED IN THIS BOOK

This list details all the major acronyms used in this book to allow easy reference. For details of their *meanings* see the Glossary (Appendix 2) or the relevant chapters.

AI	Artificial Intelligence
AKO	A-Kind-Of
ATN	Augmented Transition Network
BASIC	Beginner's All-Purpose Symbolic Instruction Code
BNF	Backus-Naur Form
CD	Conceptual Depedency
DBMS	Database Management System
DCG	Definite Clause Grammar
FOL	First Order Logic
FOPC	First Order Predicate Calculus
FSD	Finite State Diagram
GPSG	Generalised Phrase-Structure Grammar
I/O	Input and Output
KR	Knowledge Representation
KRL	Knowledge Representation Language
MOPS	Memory Organisation Packet
MUD	Multi-User Dungeons
NL	Natural Language
NPC	Non-Player Character
PSG	Phrase-Structure Grammar
RAM	Random Access Memory
RTN	Recursive Transition Network
TG	Tranformational Grammar

INDEX

SOFTWARE AVAILABLE FROM CENTURY COMMUNICATIONS

THE FOURTH PROTOCOL: The Game
(Commodore 64/ Spectrum)
Frederick Forsyth

THE CENTURY TYPING TUTOR
(Commodore 64)
Peter Lupton & Frazer Robinson

LEGEND
(Spectrum)
John Lambshead & Gordon Paterson

THE HORSE LORD
(BBC)
Jonathan Griffiths

For further details of any of the above write to:

Century Communications Ltd
Portland House
12–13 Greek Street
London W1V 5LE